PRAISE FOR *COM[E...]*

In a culture where moving and s[...] are praised, Hannah Brencher ca[...] work of staying and anchoring. Raw, relatable, and open-hearted, *Come Matter Here* will help you answer the questions of purpose, belonging, and identity with the compassion and humor of a best friend. Hannah leads a wide-open, deeply rooted life, and she is a trustworthy guide to help you do the hard work of digging in, building home, and steadily walking the path of obedience. If you're tired of running and ready to come out of hiding into the light of belonging, this book is for you.

Shelley Giglio, chief strategist, sixstepsrecords, and
cofounder, Passion Conferences/Choice Ministries

No one, and I mean *no one*, can put into words the aches, exclamations, and musings of an every-girl heart wrought with love and faith and pain quite like Hannah Brencher can. Her first book shook me to my core, made me reach deeper inside myself than I ever dreamed I could . . . to pull out this crazy zest for ordinary life, this insatiable love for other people. And with her incredible new book, she's pushed me to take another step toward *knowing* myself. I want to stand up and cheer at all of her words and, at the same time, wipe those feels-good-to-cry tears from my eyes, because reading those words on these pages—she *knows me.* And it feels so good be known. To belong. Thank goodness for the way God has used Hannah's words and pain and joy. *Come Matter Here* is one of those books I will set aside for my own daughter one day as she embarks on her own life, looking for a place to belong.

Emily Ley, author of *Grace Not
Perfection* and *A Simplified Life*

Come Matter Here is the anthem we've been desperately craving—an invitation to start living right where we are. Hannah Brencher's story, masterful writing, and passionate guidance will help us leave behind the lie that life is going to happen *someday*. It's here. You're here. And as Hannah boldly and lovingly tells readers, "I hope you know how much it matters that you're here." If you've been looking for a push to live on purpose instead of by accident, and a trusted friend to lead you down that life-giving path, you're about to discover both in these pages. *Come Matter Here* is a must-read!

Lara Casey, author of *Make It Happen* and *Cultivate*

I'm grateful for the powerful message Hannah Brencher shares in *Come Matter Here*. This book masterfully encourages us to stop chasing a level of success, happiness, or a single moment to finally believe we matter. If you're exhausted from constantly chasing the next best thing to make you feel complete, this book will help you courageously step into the journey you're on today. Hannah is not only an exceptional writer, but she truly lives out this message. She makes every person she meets feel known, accepted, and as though they were made for more right where they are. Well done!

Tyler Reagin, president of Catalyst

Words can be wings or weights. Hannah Brencher has given her readers words to lift us up and give us a space to think, but, more importantly, a space to belong. With simple yet profound truths, Hannah vulnerably takes us on her personal journey while encouraging us to discover our own. I cannot wait to share this book with my friends and remind them, "You matter here!"

Bianca Juarez Olthoff, speaker, advocate, and
bestselling author of *Play with Fire*

By vulnerably inviting her community into her darkest moments, Hannah Brencher inspires me to do the same with my own life and reminds me that there's so much beauty in letting people in.

Branden Harvey, founder of the Goodnewspaper

This book is a wakeup call—to stop waiting for future fulfillment, to stop striving for someday, and to dig deep into the moments that matter. Hannah Brencher's stories have a way of taking us by the hand and guiding us toward our truth. She doesn't shy away from the hardships of life, sharing from her own experiences of pain and redemption. This book is a resounding reminder that there is purpose in the present.

Natalie Franke, cofounder of the Rising Tide Society

For the searchers, the wanderers, the hopers, and somedayers: here, a road map.

Erin Loechner, author of *Chasing Slow*

For all of us who feel like we're always only as good as our latest win shared on social media, with a finish line always just out of reach, Hannah Brencher's words will wash over you in waves with a permission to slow down and dig deeper in a world that is always running. You'll be reminded that you were created for more than a highlight-reel kind of life and that your greatest work comes from the consistent act of showing up for people over and over again. For all of us who long to matter but are tired of running, this is the anthem we've been waiting for.

Mary Marantz, writer, speaker, entrepreneur and CEO of Black Tie Media

Come Matter Here is a truth bomb dropped into a society that has no idea how badly it needs this declaration. Hannah Brencher has crafted, beautifully and humbly, a message of calm in the chaos. Like an inhaler to an asthmatic, *Come Matter Here* is the breath we all need.

Carlos Whittaker, speaker and author of
Kill the Spider and *Moment Maker*

Come Matter Here is a triumph of truth over lies and healing over pain. The world is a better place because Hannah Brencher is in it, and this book is absolutely brilliant. You will love it and never be the same after reading it.

Alli Worthington, author of *Fierce Faith*:
*A Woman's Guide to Fighting Fear, Wrestling
Worry, and Overcoming Anxiety*

come matter here

Your Invitation to

BE HERE in a

GETTING THERE World

HANNAH BRENCHER

ZONDERVAN

Come Matter Here
Copyright © 2018 by Hannah Brencher

Requests for information should be addressed to:
Zondervan, *3900 Sparks Dr. SE, Grand Rapids, Michigan 49546*

Library of Congress Cataloging-in-Publication Data

Names: Brencher, Hannah, author.
Title: Come matter here : your invitation to be here in a getting there world /
    Hannah Brencher.
Description: Grand Rapids, Michigan : Zondervan, [2018]
Identifiers: LCCN 2018000554| ISBN 9780310350842 (softcover) | ISBN
    9780310350859 (ebook)
Subjects: LCSH: Christian life. | Brencher, Hannah. | Awareness—Religious
    aspects—Christianity.
Classification: LCC BV4501.3 .B74725 2018 | DDC 248.4—dc23 LC record
    available at https://lccn.loc.gov/2018000554

Published in association with the Stuart Krichevsky Literary Agency, Inc.,
6 East 39th Street, Suite 500, New York, NY 10016.

Cover design: connie gabbert | design & illustration
Interior design: Kait Lamphere

First printing March 2018 / Printed in the United States of America

For a dedicated group of people who
loved me back to health—
thank you for staying.

"She made unshakable commitments in all directions."

David Brooks, speaking of Dorothy Day

CONTENTS

CONTENTS

FOREWORD

"I think it is a lifelong quest to differentiate our feelings from the plans of God."

That's one of the sentences you're going to want to underline in the first chapter. If you're anything like me, I'd make sure you have three pens at least lined up to read this book. There's nothing worse than starting with one pen to make notes or doodle in exclamation marks and have to switch to another halfway through.

The first time I met Hannah Brencher was in 2015. We were both speaking at a conference, and I arrived at the event feeling pretty sick. I was trying to power through, pretending I wasn't as sick as I knew I was, since I really wanted to be there—and specifically wanted to hear what God had to say through her.

The day I left and the days that followed were pretty traumatic. I don't remember much of the plane ride home, except for being violently ill. I literally can't remember large chunks of time that followed in the forty-eight hours after I made it back to my city, because as it turns out, I had viral meningitis. The good news is that I infected no one at the event and eventually made a full recovery; the bad news is that I had a crazy serious illness and spent the following week in the hospital and the weeks after that really sick and bedridden.

I don't remember a lot from the conference due to the meningitis, but I remember Hannah.

I remember passing her as she sat alone in a sunny spot reading her Bible. There are flashes of visual memories stashed in my brain of Hannah listening intently to others. I remember her sitting erect and engaged on the edge of the stage, passionately conveying what God had put on her heart to share. And I remember a friend of hers commenting on her growth and vulnerability and wisdom, saying, "Hannah used to tell stories. Now . . . she testifies."

Feelings are important, as are the plans and truths of God. You're going to come face-to-face with both in this book. You'll confront your own feelings, which will absolutely be evoked by her honest stories, and you'll also be exposed, in the best way, to the eternal perspective of a good and loving Father God who is *for* you and *after* you in the most beautiful ways. You'll be exposed to the only true path toward mattering, and it may force you to leave all other paths behind.

Hannah is a great storyteller, but that's not what she's doing here. She's testifying.

Remember that I warned you about having three pens ready. You're going to need them.

Jess Connolly

BEFORE ANYTHING ELSE

I have a friend, Blake, who reminds me of a younger version of myself.

I met him through my church in Atlanta. Blake is likable and personable; he's not afraid to be real with you. He has a massive heart and loves to call out the greatness in other people.

When I first met Blake, we were sitting in a conference room tucked off to the side of the building where I rented desk space. A long wooden table sat between us. I asked Blake questions about himself to get to know him better, about his hopes and his pursuits. Yet I felt like there was a barrier between us as we talked. His answers seemed polished, as if he had lined up all the stories he was going to tell that day before meeting up with me.

"Blake," I interrupted him at one point, "tell me something real."

I didn't expect to say that, but the words came tumbling out of my mouth before I could stop them. I don't know how to do much small talk. I think life is incredibly short, and so I want to get to the heart of things pretty quickly, preferably in the first five minutes of knowing someone.

"I mean, tell me something a lot of people don't really know about you," I said. He looked at me, and then he looked down.

I could see him thinking the words over in his head before he said them.

"You know, I wake up every single day wondering if any of this is worth it." He motioned around the conference room. I could tell he meant all of life—the waking up, the going places, the meeting people. All of it.

"I go to sleep by the light of my phone, looking at all the places I've mattered throughout a day. It only fills me for a few minutes before I need something else."

He said, "I knew all day that you and I had this meeting, and so I waited all day to hear from you so I could get up, get dressed, and go matter somewhere."

He was quiet for a minute and then said something that changed everything for me.

"I'm almost always waiting on a text from someone that reads, 'Come matter here.'"

Come matter here. I know that story. I lived that story. For years, I was consumed by what it would mean to "matter" in this world. To people. To someone special. To God.

I think we've all felt that. We want to know that our lives matter, that this isn't some crazy accident we all got stuck inside of. I started to chase after whatever the world told me mattered. Success. Acclaim. Love. Happiness. I became obsessed with this idea of "getting there," wherever "there" was. I was in a constant state of waiting to arrive somewhere better.

I didn't know yet that all the good things—like faith, love, trust—don't happen overnight. You can't pick them up from the drive-thru or snag them in an instant download. It's easier to run after the next thing the world tells you matters. It's easier to never do the hard work of planting your roots or letting people in as you grab your suitcase and run hard toward "the next thing."

But when you get tired of running, there's a better story waiting to begin. I promise, it's better. Yet there's a catch: you'll just have to stick around long enough. You'll have to dig in and do the work—the work that happens in the *here and now*.

| *Chapter One* | # BE WHERE YOUR FEET ARE |

I spent the last hours of 2013 sitting on the floor of my friend's New York City apartment surrounded by pictures of tiny copper teakettles. It had become a tradition for a bunch of friends to gather on the Upper West Side on the afternoon of New Year's Eve and make vision boards for the year ahead. We haul in magazines we've saved throughout the year and spend a few hours reflecting and dreaming up what we hope to make happen in the new year.

December 31 has always been my favorite day of the year. I start celebrating early in the morning and let the festivities of a New Year drag on until about the middle of March. I think there's something really beautiful about the last day of the year. There's an anticipation hanging in the air, an infectious energy buzzing around because on this day—and sometimes only on this one day out of 365—people genuinely believe they can do better. They can be better.

The two years before this one, my vision boards were always full of images and words placed strategically to make me want to hustle, move, and shake up the world. There would be multiple suitcases and verbs like "RUN" or "GO" spread out across the board. I don't think there's anything wrong with wanting to do something that matters, but I do think it's dangerous to center all our decisions around being enough for the world.

19

This year, I couldn't stop reaching for the home and living magazines. I couldn't explain why my hands kept grabbing for them or why I kept ripping out pictures of dishes. And teacups. And chairs. And adorable office spaces. And white linens.

"It looks like I am building a home this year," I announced to my friends around the room, all hunched over their own pieces of poster board. "I didn't even think I wanted this."

A home seemed out of place in my current lifestyle. I'd made a lot of things happen in the last year. I'd contracted and written a book. I'd traveled around the country giving talks to big audiences. I had pieces of my writing go viral. I was doing everything I thought I was supposed to be doing. This was the stuff the world told me mattered. This was the stuff people always wanted to talk about, how they could climb higher too.

Yet the more I did, the more restless I found myself. I kept thinking if I could just fill this growing hole inside me with something greater, then I would feel full. It was always one big "then," but never anything I actually arrived at. I was starting to wonder if the hole would ever be filled, or if there was another road I wasn't taking yet toward something totally different but something completely better.

When you only focus on the life you project to the world, you start living halfheartedly. It becomes nearly impossible to be content with the life you have. Instead, you run the rat race of always chasing after that "next thing" to temporarily fill you or allow you to impress people a little longer.

I picked up another magazine and began flipping through the contents. I opened to a two-page spread with the words "SWEET GEORGIA MAY" plastered in big white letters across it.

"Georgia." "May." There was another reminder, just like the dozen or so I had gotten in the last few months since I made the decision to move to Georgia that coming May. I was in the process of writing my first book, and I knew it would be completed by May. It was my third year of working for myself. I'd built a steady income doing freelance writing, ghostwriting, and speaking at colleges and conferences. I had nothing tying me to one specific place on the map. For some people, that would be the ultimate adventure. This reality terrified me. I never thought I'd be someone to pick up and move to a new place.

Atlanta seems like a really random place to want to move to. In actuality, I became friends with a girl named Eryn, who lived just outside of Atlanta. We technically met in person once before in New York City, but neither of us could recall it, so I say the first time we really spoke was over the phone after Eryn asked if we could connect. We were both young women hustling to make the world better through small businesses, and she expressed how lonely that could sometimes be. I knew the feeling, so I jumped at the chance to talk with her.

By the end of the conversation, Eryn was inviting me to visit the South for the first time. I don't know if she expected me to take her up on the offer, but I booked the plane ticket the next week and flew into Atlanta a few months later. It was there, throughout a whole week with her, that I felt a real urgency to be there. I wanted to stay longer. I wanted to meet more people. I wanted to figure out if I belonged in this place, if I could build a life here.

That became the first of many trips to Georgia, one of them being a road trip with a girl who wasn't my friend before the road trip. We met at a party in Connecticut and bonded over our love for Georgia and sweet tea. She'd grown up in Georgia, and she mentioned that her grandmother still lived there, in a wooded cabin in the northern mountains. By the end of the night, we'd planned a road trip to go visit Grandma.

Our plans came together so suddenly that I ended up texting her the night before the trip and asking, "So wait, are we really going?"

A few hours later, before the sun came up, we packed up her car and made the fourteen-hour journey down southern highways. We brought a banjo to sing songs along the way, though neither of us knew how to actually play the instrument. We tacked a few hours on to our road trip, stopping at every cheesy attraction plastered on the billboards.

We stayed with her grandmother in the woods and got adopted by her Southern lake family for the Fourth of July weekend. This feeling of being welcomed in and wanted enveloped me tighter than the Georgia humidity, and I felt home. We rode around the Atlanta interstates, wearing snapbacks and flip-flops, talking to Southern guys on Tinder, asking ourselves if we could really live here. Atlanta and her people validated this strong voice in my head that always wanted the courage to be able to say, *There is a place for you here. You belong in places that know your name and places that don't yet know you're coming for them.*

I used to think you needed to leave if you wanted to change your life or try something different. I thought geography could heal the mess that comes from being human—like a clean slate. We all want different things that keep us coming and going and staying and living.

———

I used to say I moved to Atlanta because God told me to move there. I think we need to be really careful when we say, "God told me to . . .," because, a lot of times, we equate our own feelings about a situation with requests that God makes to us. Just because I feel something may not mean God is confirming it. I think it is a lifelong quest to differentiate our feelings from the plans of God.

Even with the hope that I would end up back in Atlanta, it wasn't enough for me to pack my suitcase and just go. I was struck with a fear of making a wrong move. This fear has been a plaguing factor in my young adult life. I think we invest crazy amounts of energy into whether or not we are supposed to do something. I have a friend named Luke who says we waste too much time waiting for direction from God. We run around frantically asking for signs. We act as though the apocalypse is upon us. I don't think it matters so much if you can't figure out whether or not God wanted you to break up with that person, whether or not God wanted you in that city. Luke says we are all waiting for some "big reveal"—and what if it's not some big reveal? What if it's just a lot of work and choices, the slow, slow work of building the muscle of discernment?

I dated a guy for a short period of time who always wanted to define the relationship after every date we went on. It was endearing for a little while. He would plan creative dates, like a picnic in the park or a late-night diner trip to eat breakfast for dinner. I stopped wanting to go because I knew the conversation would come as he drove me home.

"Okay, so where are we now?" He always wanted to keep his pulse on every moment, and it made it hard to just relax and go with the flow.

It didn't really give me freedom for feelings to develop on

their own. It just kept me in a constant state of waiting for that next "define the relationship" talk.

In a lot of ways, I'm the dude constantly wanting to define the relationship, and God is the person in the passenger seat who is just hoping we can get home without me asking, "So where are we now?"

I used to constantly pray for direction and signs. I felt like I was really bad at this whole faith thing because I couldn't trust God, but then I encountered Moses. Moses really couldn't move two steps without needing God to assure him, remind him, and coax him into the right places. At some points, you want to be, like, "Moses, dude, just do the thing!" At other points, I think it's really beautiful to need God that much, to trust God's direction above my own.

I expect God to be like Siri, telling me where to turn and when. Instead, I get these vague promptings or these tiny moments you can easily overlook if you aren't paying attention to them.

I think if God and I were texting buddies, he would send me messages on the regular that read, "Calm down. Stop asking for signs. Just be here now. You are going to miss life if you keep asking me if you are in the right place. You're here. That's all that matters. Be where your feet are."

Here's what I think God does: he uses our decisions to teach us something, move us closer to him, and do whatever he can to make us better versions of ourselves. That's the mission that God has for our little lives: that we become less selfish, less absorbed with our own thoughts, less critical, less negative, and ultimately happier because of all the "less." God is not a god of self-improvement, but he is a God who knows that if we could just get out of our own way—just stop thinking the world revolves around us—we would be so much happier and the world would be so much better off. God uses cities, death, and birth to make us better versions of ourselves, but his most preferred method to change people is through other people.

———————

I prayed for a sign one morning about moving to Atlanta, and shortly after the prayer had ended, my phone beeped. I had a new email. I opened my inbox to find an email with the subject line "Be where your feet are" waiting for me.

It was from a reader named Katie. She was a senior in college who was living in an off-campus apartment for her final year of college. She and her roommates were just four months from graduation. After that, everything would change. They would go to different places in the world. They would undoubtedly go on to great things. But the "here" they created would never again exist.

She wrote to tell me their motto for the year was just that: *be where your feet are.* I think that's what I struggle with the most. It's hard to be "here" when there are a million little things pushing us to be somewhere else. We always want to be hustling toward "the next big thing." The next thing to make us feel more impressive or seen. I thought these next big things would fill us, but I think they make us hungrier for bigger things.

So there I was, praying for God to give me a sign that I would be in the right place, and an email with the message "be where your feet are" appropriately showed up in my inbox. No surprise. Presence is all we get at any given moment. We either lean into the here and now, or we miss it.

I think something bigger is always happening, but it is never how we narrate it in our own head. It never is. We will meet people we never imagined in places we never planned to go. But it starts with a choice and then follows with a step. Make a choice. Take a step. Make a choice. Take a step. It's a rhythm of life. You may not get your answer until you make the choice and take the step.

———————

I think we all want to get to the place where we belong. Even the most adventurous people reach a point where they decide they want to settle down and have a place to call "home."

I wrestled with that term *home* when Atlanta started showing up, because I technically had one. I had everything I was supposed to want—the support of my parents, good girlfriends, a church, a coworking space to work out of, and a boyfriend.

Caleb was such a decisive person, and that's what I loved most about him. He was employed, owned a house, and had benefits. I was twenty-five—the age where throw pillows and health insurance suddenly became sexy to me.

It probably would have been easier to keep my eyes on Georgia if our time spent getting to know one another wasn't him picking me up in his pickup truck to go feed the homeless on a cold November night or organizing fleeces and windbreakers at a coat drive the day before Thanksgiving. As he showed me his Mother Teresa status, I found myself wondering if this is what I'd been waiting for.

He said on one of our first dates that we didn't have to do this—this dating thing—if I was planning on leaving. I probably figured he'd go along with my indecision and then follow me to Georgia, like some great romantic comedy. Just the opposite, the man was saying to me, "I don't want to date you if you're going to run from being rooted."

So I lied to him and stopped talking about Atlanta. I decided I would stay. I would make us work.

I remember one specific night with Caleb when we decided to hang out, go to the mall to buy him shoes, and make salads. We were lying on the couch, laughing over something I can't remember, and he blurted out, "I've fallen really hard for you."

My body froze up in that moment. I looked at him. Blinked twice. In all the time we'd been dating, I kept waiting to fall. I was doing virtually everything possible to force myself to fall. To no avail, I was completely grounded.

"I guess we just fall in different ways," I said to him, suddenly feeling guilty. Right then and there, my Hallmark line of awkward breakup cards was born.

I thought I dodged the bullet when we didn't say anything more on the matter, but as we were walking into the grocery store a few hours later, he brought it up again.

"What did you mean earlier?"

"Earlier?"

"Yeah," he said. "You said earlier, 'I guess we just fall in different ways.' What did you mean by that?"

I didn't answer him. We didn't speak as we meandered through the aisles of the grocery store picking up croutons and carrots. And then we got to the salad dressing aisle. And the salad dressing aisle is the worst place in the world to be when you are already having a tough time making a decision about your life, your boyfriend, and your geographic location.

We stopped in front of the display of Ranch and Caesar and stood silently.

"Pick one," he said to me. His voice was distant and quiet.

"I don't have a preference," I said to him. "I want whichever one you want."

"No," he said. "You know which one you want. So pick it."

He lingered for a moment and then left me standing in the middle of the aisle as he walked toward the registers. I knew we weren't talking about honey mustard anymore. It wasn't about the salad dressing. It was about the fact that we wanted different things and that's okay. I wanted a suitcase and he wanted a life.

Back at his house that evening, with empty salad bowls by our feet, I really tried to articulate my thoughts to him—the truth that I actually wasn't uncertain; I was just afraid. I was afraid that if I chose to leave, I would miss something. I was constantly afraid that God was holding out two options and asking me to pick the better one. The God of my brain at this point resembled Regina George from the movie *Mean Girls*, always waiting for me to slip up and fail. I was afraid that at one point soon, I would make the wrong choice and the game would stop, just like it does on *The Price is Right* when a contestant guesses the wrong unit price for the dish detergent.

I was trying to make out the words, and then I was crying. I was crying hard. Caleb reached for my hand and pulled me off the couch and into the kitchen. He opened the cabinet door where he kept his dinner plates. He pulled out the big white stack of them. All of them. And he led me down to the basement. He set the dishes on the floor and then pulled the first one off the top and handed it to me.

"Here," he said. "Break it."

"Break it?" I said. "Your plates?"

"It's just dishes. I can get more."

A few weeks earlier, I'd told him about a TV show I saw where the girl goes through a breakup and her mother takes her to this old warehouse where they got to throw plates against a wall to let all their indecision and heartbreak out. Now here we were, in his basement, wearing glasses to play it safe as we broke all his dinner plates before breaking up. We took turns winging each plate into the floor, watching them explode into pieces like a porcelain fireworks show. We were laughing like we'd gone mad. It was the most at ease with us I'd ever felt.

I laughed to the point where I was crying again. I don't think he noticed the tears streaming down my face as I whipped dinner plates into the concrete basement floor. I was angry with God because I didn't understand. I didn't understand why people walked into our lives and swept us up with romantic gestures and then we let them go. I was afraid, more than anything, that I would never meet the person who is right for me. Maybe I would always be waiting to fall for the good guys but always falling when the wrong person is there to catch me.

As he swept the pieces of the broken plates into the corner, Caleb had a somber look on his face. He was full of joy five minutes before, but now he looked gutted.

"What's wrong?" I asked him.

"I'm just waiting for you to see it," he said to me.

"See what?"

"See that this is all I can offer you. You want to go out there and do big things, and you will. But this is all I can offer you." He motioned to show the basement, the foundation of a home, a life he built before I showed up. He'd done the work.

He'd made the choices. And now what he wanted more than anything was for someone to stay with him in those choices and help him keep building.

Our breakup a week later was clean and not dramatic. It was bittersweet clarity. When a breakup is clean, the reality is clear: you are going to love somebody else one day and so will the other person. It will all, hopefully, be beautiful. And so, out of respect for the people who are coming next, you both grow up and let go. I wanted a suitcase and he wanted a rooted life.

We admitted that we wanted different things. No one was at fault. You're allowed to want different things, and those different things might be the defining reason you need to leave. I told him he restored my hope, that I'd never had the standard of a guy opening my car doors until him and that I planned to keep it. He thanked me too.

"I think you are going to Georgia," he said to me before we hung up.

"I think so too," I told him. "I think so too."

When my mom was twenty-three, she broke off an engagement, packed up her life, and moved across the country to New Mexico, where she spent time working at an orphanage and finding herself and God. I loved this story for a long time and romanticized it to all of my friends until I got the details straight. My mom was telling me the details all along, but I wasn't listening to them. I was hearing exactly what I wanted to hear: woman breaks herself free with an "I don't need no man" ballad, charges into the world, helps humanity, and makes her own love story. I've seen this movie dozens of times at this point.

My mother's story is beautiful, but it's not without heart-break and a lot of messy stuff. She had to send her wedding gifts back. The man she was going to marry died tragically in a motorcycle accident a few years later. Hours before his wake, she realized she didn't have any respectable clothes to wear, and that was her wake-up call: *Get some real clothes and grow up, girl.* She moved to New Mexico and worked at a home for runaways. She went from partying a lot to partying a moderate amount to partying less and searching more. She and God were on a "maybe I'll text you back" basis. She didn't want God if he wanted to change her. Somewhere under the New Mexico sun, she grew into a person who would eventually move back to where the whole journey started—with a stronger faith than she ever imagined—and meet the man who would eventually become my father.

I think we worship these stories of leaving it all behind and going somewhere new, but I'm beginning to see that every one of those stories has the same truth holding up this romantic idea of leaving: The stuff you're not facing will follow you. It will get in the car too. It will pack a bag too. Leaving isn't the key; changing is. I'm learning that life isn't about the destinations we can boast about getting to; it's about all the walking in between that feels pointless when you try to take a picture of it because no one will understand it like you do. It's the in between stuff that fleshes out a story—gives it guts and transformation.

It's not about the scenery changing or the person you say good night to. The traveler must be the one to change. That's what makes the story good.

STEAL THIS PRAYER

Dear God, teach me to be here now. Not ten years in the past or five years in the future. Help me to look up and look around at the people in my life and the things you're asking me to do. I want to live in the present moment. Please root me in the here and now.

Chapter Two	# BUILD OUT OF LOVE INSTEAD

Not long ago, I shot a video with a tissue company. It was a divine partnership because I cry all the time. They followed me around town and had me hold tissues while I talked to the camera about sending love letters to people in need. A lot of people associate love letters with tissues apparently. A whole crew showed up to my office space to conduct the interview.

A producer on the crew named Jenny had a "mild" obsession with Elvis. It came out when we went across the street to grab a quick lunch and she made the comment, "Oh, Elvis would have loved this place. They serve his favorite kind of sandwich."

She was talking about the king of rock 'n' roll. Whom she had never met. I would learn in the next few hours that she had Elvis tattoos, a child named after Elvis, and an Elvis car (among other Elvis things). The only time in the span of the whole day when Jenny didn't talk about Elvis was when the cameraman was interviewing me.

"Now, I don't want you to look at the camera," he said to me. "I want you to look at Jenny the whole time."

The cameraman began asking me questions and I kept reminding myself to focus on Jenny. It was a pretty weird situation to be talking at someone who wasn't supposed to say anything back to you. It feels really vulnerable to open up your heart without being able to take your eyes off someone. At one point, I was staring at Jenny and tears were streaming down her face. She looked away from me and off toward the corner of the room.

People always say it's best to acknowledge the elephant in the room. Well, there was an Elvis in the room that day that she and I never acknowledged. There was something about this woman, just below the surface of our conversations, that I couldn't quite pin down. I wanted to ask her more questions. I wanted to switch the interview onto her. I wanted to know why she talked about Elvis so much and what she would choose to talk about if I asked her about something more than velvet suits.

I think every one of our stories has some sort of Elvis standing in the middle of it, keeping us from telling the real story, the thing happening just below the surface.

For me, it's always been fear. I've wrestled all my life with what to name it, so I'm just calling it fear. Some people call it anxiety. Other people call it ego. Fear, I've learned, is the thing that wants to keep us in our comfort zone. Fear is the ultimate desire to stay safe.

My fear, for as long as I can remember, was all-encompassing though. Fear wrote emails for me. Fear went on dates for me. Fear told me what I could and could not do. I listened to fear because its voice became as common as a friend you eat lunch with every day. It wasn't a healthy voice, but it was familiar.

I'm going to use fear and anxiety interchangeably for the next few sentences. Like Clark Kent and Superman—same dude, different operating hours. The thing is, no one ever told me about anxiety or fear growing up. It never got a name. And like most things with no name, it became more powerful than it had to be in my life. It's like this documentary I watched on Netflix about a girl who found out over the internet that she had a twin sister, someone who was separated from her at birth, living in a different country. That discovery changed everything for her. Suddenly, she had a sister. That sister had a name. In a similar way, I wish someone had sat me down when I was younger and said something like, "Hey, you have anxiety. That's its name. Anxiety can spiral into depression. It runs in your family on both sides."

Anxiety, I've learned, is like an overzealous Monopoly player, except its playing board is your brain. It wants to build houses and hotels all over your territories—your relationships, your job, your health, your spirituality. One of the hardest things to learn is that not everything anxiety tells you is true.

I bring up so much about fear because it is likely a part of your story. I find fear chillin' like a villain in the voices of so many of my friends who wonder if they should go after that thing, chase that dream, move to that city, pursue that person. If we aren't careful, fear will take over our lives with a Stephen King agenda, ready to write a horrific thriller where a love story always belonged. Fear builds a road map when we aren't looking.

When I decided to actually move to Atlanta (like actually, actually move and not just talk about it), I let it be quiet news that only I knew for a few days. I was more afraid I would turn back or find another reason to stay. I let the thrill of the idea wear off until all that was left was the reality and the fear.

When you make any sort of big decision, there's the initial twenty-four-hour high that comes from doing something brave, followed by a sinking, doubting feeling. Fear rolls up with a posse more intimidating than the twenty-six women emerging out of limos on the first episode of a new *Bachelor* season. You start to go back on yourself. Something inside you seems to whisper, *You can't do this. You're not actually made for this.* Too much of the time, we pause, agree with the whisper, and then retreat to a more comfortable space.

If I could write an autobiography for fear, it would read like this:

Hi, my name is Fear. F-E-A-R. But you are going to call me a lot of other things as you start to get closer to me. I'm terribly unoriginal. I'm like every has-been out there, but you give me way more credit than I deserve. You should keep doing that. I like it when you make me bigger than I actually am. I'm going to make you feel alone, and I like it when you believe you're the only one who's ever felt this way. You think I'm custom-catered to fit you, but I'm really no different than the brand of me your best friend wears. I'm a ballad lurking in the hearts of a billion people, and I will do anything to keep you from realizing that I am just the same song on repeat. You all know all my words.

I'm pretty jealous though. I want you alone with me at night. I'm not afraid to say I'm greedy or that I don't want to share you. I'm a territorial lover, and I would rather you not have solid and deep conversations at dinner parties or find a community that doesn't leave your side. I wrote you a story a long time ago, and I don't want you to figure out that you've outgrown the plotline.

I wonder why you don't get over me sometimes, but then the realization hits me: You come back because you know I want you. You come back because you know the sound of my voice. You come

back because you know the way I move and how I shut you down.
You've stood face-to-face with me so many times and I have told you
who you are. The crazy thing is, you've believed me.

———————

Things fell into place pretty quickly once I opened myself up to the idea of actually going through with the move. I found a space to rent an office to continue doing my freelance work. Eryn came alongside and connected me with a girl named Morgan, who was looking for a roommate. She was renting a two-bedroom bungalow in Atlanta and thought we might get along. In a matter of a day, I was on the phone with Morgan and confirming that I would be coming to live with her that May—two months from then.

I told one friend I was leaving. Just one. Her name is Lindsey, and I honestly don't know how I became close with her because she has four children under the age of five and barely any free time.

She invited me over the evening I told her. I sat on her couch and she let me know she thought I needed to leave too. She also told me that moving, going somewhere to build a new life, would be harder than I thought.

"I've been praying about you. Really, I've been escaping to the bathroom to pray for you because I can't do much of anything with four humans needing me to keep them alive at every second of the day," she said. I pictured Lindsey holed up in the bathroom on her knees while the kids scratched at the door.

Lindsey is someone who has consistently prayed for me at every transition I've been through since I've gotten to know her. Her prayers often sound like she's reading my palm because she can see things that are coming in the future and she's yet to be wrong.

"As I was praying for you, I kept thinking, *God is going to do a lot of things when you get to Georgia*," she said. "He is going to strip you and gut you. This will be your refining fire."

These aren't exactly the encouraging words you imagine someone saying to you when you tell them you're moving somewhere new. It just fills my mind with this awful image of God and me having a fistfight in a back alley and God, because he's God, wins. It makes me think of suffering. We don't welcome suffering in our culture. We don't even really talk about it. We want to skip over the parts of the Bible where suffering actually turns us into better versions of ourselves.

It reminds me of Tim Keller's wise insight in which he said, "If you believe in Jesus and rest in him, then suffering will relate to your character like fire relates to gold."[1] He's saying the stuff we'd rather not walk through will be the things that define us, make us, transform us, and turn us into gold. That's what happens in the refining fire—gold may come out of it, but gold cannot exist without the flames.

"I feel like this refining is going to happen in a really safe space," Lindsey continued. "It's going to be hard, but you're going to be surrounded as it is happening."

I was scared of what she meant by this. I had these really whimsical views about moving to Atlanta. I pictured myself in a cute house with lots of Southern friends. I imagined I'd be successful and drink lots of sweet tea. I felt like I would find

---

1. Tim Keller, *Walking with God through Pain and Suffering* (New York: Dutton, 2013), 234.

a new home and it would be easy, but Lindsey was telling me, "Just the opposite, girl. You don't find a home; you build it."

"I want you to look around," she said. "Look at all the things you've done here. You've built so many beautiful things, but you built them all out of fear.

"I just don't want you to think you have to go through your entire life being ruled by fear," she continued. "It wouldn't be too big to believe you could let the fear go. You could build out of love instead."

I used to think the goal was to be fearless, to reach the point in my faith where nothing could scare me. I don't believe that anymore. While I don't want to live my life paralyzed by fear, I think it can be healthy in doses. Fear wakes us up. Fear reminds us to fight. It's only when we know fear that we ever understand the depth of our need for its opposite—love. Real love. Hard, rich, durable love.

Fear can either keep us standing in one place, or it can propel us toward something better. At my last dance recital before graduating from high school, my tap teacher gave me a poster with a butterfly printed on it. The quote below the image read, "You must be willing to surrender who you are for what you could become." Despite the cheesy photo of the butterfly emerging from a cocoon, I really liked the quote.

I think the caterpillar-turned-butterfly analogy is cheesy, but I read in a book a while back how some caterpillars go through a stage called "diapause" where instead of undergoing the transformation of becoming a butterfly, they decide to hold off until the following spring. The author explained it as a "clinging state"—a caterpillar holding tight to its old life for a little while longer. They resist because of the circumstances around them. I like to imagine these caterpillars are just like us, having no idea what could be on the other side of this transformation and finding it hard to believe there could actually be something better at the end of themselves.

It's a state of clinging. A state of unrest. We go through it too. There is something inside us that rises up and begs to hold on to what we know, to what is most familiar to us. We try to resist change. We look for people to be our lifeboats. We look to fear in the hope that it will keep us safe. We hate the fact that darkness could be good for us. We all want the chance to be gold, but we don't want the fire.

I don't have to tell you how the rest of the story goes. You already know what happens to those caterpillars when they just let go.

STEAL THIS PRAYER

Dear God, it's hard not to hand the pen to fear and let it write the story for me. Take back the pen and rewrite my story with a better narrative. Wipe out my fears and squash their credibility. Give me the courage to build out of love instead.

| *Chapter Three* | # OCCUPY NEW SPACE |

Two months later, I am a resident of Atlanta. I pack everything I own—which isn't much—into my Toyota Camry with windows so tinted only a drug dealer could love them. My mom tucks a love letter into one of my bags, a ritual she's created over the years with every good-bye we've said. I say my weepy good-byes to my girlfriends one evening as they all come around me and pray. They record the prayers they're saying out loud over me so I can listen to them whenever I need encouragement or find myself getting lonely. Lindsey has me over one last time before I leave. She hands me cupcakes topped with gold flecks and a wrapped-up treasure map that's really a pencil case. It's a reminder to me to go and find the gold.

I get into my car and start the sixteen-hour journey to Atlanta. In my mind, I'm thinking this is all the journey will be—sixteen hours. One car ride. Like somehow the anxiety will just fall off me and out of the car somewhere in the middle of Virginia, and I'll cross over the Georgia line as a new person. As I drive, I think about a conversation I had with my friend Drue right before I left.

She and I were standing in the kitchen, leaning against the refrigerator as we talked. It was Saint Patrick's Day, so it was like we could hear the sounds of a homemade Gaelic band in the background, complete with ukulele and tambourine.

"When we moved in the past, we did so begrudgingly," she told me. "It's like we knew we were supposed to move but we acted like it was a prison sentence instead of an opportunity."

Drue and her husband, Neil, have made several moves in their marriage. Two years earlier, they moved from Kansas City to Connecticut so Neil could attend graduate school at Yale. Recently he'd finished school and they were now preparing for another move to Seattle.

"We learned it's so much harder to find and establish a home when you're romanticizing what you left behind," she continued. "You can't really see a place for all it is when you're too busy thinking about where you were yesterday."

I had been starting to feel the same way, feeling like I was being pushed out. Truly, no one was pushing me out. I was making a choice to move and I was having a hard time processing the next step in that choice—the actual moving.

"Ultimately, we decided to change how we did things," Drue told me. She made a decision to never go anywhere again and not call it "home."

"When we touched down in Connecticut, we squeezed each other's hand and said, 'Welcome home.' And when we touch down in Seattle, I know God will meet us," she said to me with confidence. "We are going to squeeze each other's hand again and say first, 'Welcome home.'"

"Welcome Home." Those were the words marked in chalk on my doorstep as I arrived at the small white house with the black shutters that we would later call the Blake Bungalow. My room-mate was waiting for me so she could take me to IKEA.

IKEA furniture is of the devil. That's what I learned my first week living in Atlanta. It's the biggest lesson I can offer you.

I think the people at IKEA must get together once every quarter and ask each other, "How can we make this harder for people?"

"Oh, oh," one person pipes up in the meeting. "Let's have them figure out the stuff they want and then let's get them lost in a maze before they get to the place where they can actually pick up their stuff."

"Yes," another says. "Let's plant cinnamon buns off to the side so they'll be forced to veer off and binge in the middle of a stressful moment. Even better, let's not even give them furniture! Let's give them three boxes with fifty slabs of wood in each and then all these little pieces that may or may not even help them assemble it! And then let's put it all in Swedish."

I bet they eat cinnamon buns at these meetings. I bet none of them go home to furniture from IKEA.

For the first few nights, I screamed obscenities at the furniture. I sliced my hand open at one point and played worship music in the hope that it would make the process go smoother. I sat there on the floor of my new home in Atlanta, surrounded by a half-made dresser and desk legs, and cried. The directions didn't make sense. The map wasn't useful. I was alone, and I didn't know how to ask for help.

A few nights later, I had a speaking engagement at an event for young creative people who lived in Atlanta. I stepped onto the stage with more nerves than I had felt in a long time. This wasn't a room full of people I would never see again. I couldn't take a cab to the airport and leave directly afterward. No, this was my home now and these would be my people. I felt like I was back in fourth grade, standing before a group of my peers, begging them to pick me for their kickball team.

"I'm Hannah," I said to the room full of strangers. "And I don't have any friends and I need them. So please email me and ask me to grab coffee with you because I want to be your friend."

I aimed my clicker at the screen in back of me and my personal email address showed up in big, bold letters. I smiled at people nervously. If that introduction wasn't awkward enough, I took it a step further.

"There is IKEA furniture in my living room that I've been bleeding over trying to assemble. And since I don't have any friends, I have to ask you guys to please show up at my house and assemble this furniture with me. I'm serious. I need people to show up at my door and help me build furniture."

I thought people were going to think I was crazy, but the following day, I opened my inbox to find a dozen invitations to coffee and one email from a husband and wife with time slots for when they could come over and build furniture with me.

I picked a time slot and emailed back my address. Right on time, the two showed up at my door. He came in carrying a toolbox and I welcomed them into the wreckage of my living room.

The woman thrust a bag of coffee at me, exclaiming, "We're so happy you're here!"

"You didn't have to get me anything," I said to her. "You guys are the ones helping me. I'm supposed to be the hospitable one."

"Nonsense," she said to me. "That's just how we do it."

She isn't kidding though; that is just how people in the South do it. I've learned there are a few fantastic things ingrained in the

DNA of Southern people. Hospitality. Pride. Biscuits. Family. Porch sitting. Sweet tea. Community.

"You two sit on the couch and get to know each other," the husband said, setting down his toolbox. "I've got this covered."

For the next hour, he sat on the floor of the bungalow and assembled furniture while she and I sat on the couch with cups of tea and talked about transition. Before we reached the bottom of our mugs, I had a dresser and a desk with no missing parts to them. He moved the new furniture into my bedroom. We sat there talking for an hour longer before I walked them out and thanked them for coming over to help me.

"Welcome home," she said to me as she hugged me tight and walked out into the night to their car.

As I crawled into bed, I looked around the room that was suddenly becoming a more inviting space, more mine. I said a quick prayer. I said thank you for the desk and the dresser. I said thank you for the wave of humility washing over me and reminding me to ask for help, to just turn down the do-it-yourself Beyoncé anthem in my brain. I said thank you for the beginning because I knew one day I would look back and remember how hard it is to start rebuilding when you've already belonged somewhere else. Yet belonging isn't a destination, not a spot you can find on the map. Belonging is more like the instruction manual that comes with the IKEA furniture. It's impossible to decipher the steps at first, and you almost always want to give up trying halfway through. Turns out that belonging is a process you get to be a part of, a series of active steps that build you into someone better. Step one: go to the door and let people in.

———

The first thing I tried to do in Atlanta was find a church. I knew this would probably be the hardest decision I'd end up making. Finding a church is a personal experience. Finding a church in the Southern states is particularly difficult because there are far too many options.

One of the people I met at the speaking engagement a few days earlier invited me to go with him. We set up the time. We confirmed everything over email and he gave me his phone number in case I needed it.

The night before we were going to meet up, he got a text from a number he didn't recognize. It said, "Sorry, I won't be able to make it tomorrow." He assumed the text was from me and so he made other plans—but I hadn't been the one texting him.

I found all of this out as I was sitting in one of the back rows of this new church waiting for him to come walking through the doors. He was forty-five minutes away when we realized the miscommunication. Church was starting and I was alone. No one talked to me or said hi. Somehow I made it through the whole service without so much as a hello from anyone. I was confused. I was thinking that if there's any place where people would make you feel less alone, it's church.

I don't like attending church alone. I especially don't like it if I don't know a single person in the city. But the church was really beautiful. Like if I could mash together the feelings I get when I hear Mumford & Sons with the visuals from an Anthropologie catalog and call it *church*—it would be that kind of simple-beautiful.

I wanted to take everything in, but I kept looking at the stage and wishing I were back in a place where I knew the people with the pretty voices and could call them "friend." I kept wishing I were back in a place where I'd naturally feel someone put their arm around me in the middle of the service and it just felt safe—like I was wanted in that place. And the whispers of my heart roared, *I don't want to rebuild*.

That's what we never plan for. We plan for growth. We plan (and hope) for acceptance. We plan for abundance. We plan for friends. We plan for adventure. But we don't sit down and plan to rebuild. That was never a part of the instant plan.

It's in moments like these that you feel very small. The momentum of the move is over. The boxes are nearly unpacked. The bed is made. You've gotten a few groceries and you're relatively settled in. And then it will hit you. You are here. You made it. You don't know what's coming up next. You can't predict the future or how God will direct steps into place. It will just be you, sitting on a new mattress, in a room that's all yours. Just you in the middle of a sanctuary, crying to the music as it draws you in. Wherever you're going, tell yourself it will be good. Whoever you're going to turn into, tell yourself that person will be good too. Do your best to usher in hope where fear wants to stand.

This is a turning point, whether you see it or not yet. It's a chance to occupy new space.

Occupy new space—that's the advice I got from one of the people I met for coffee in those first few weeks in Atlanta. Her name is Nia. She sat across from me and told me about leaving a job she really loved because she realized she needed to move on. Someone else would come and fill her role. Hopefully they'd do an even better job than her.

"I needed to go out there and occupy new space," she said to me.

I loved that when she said it. It was such a cool picture in my brain. It's this hope that we will all go out there and fill up the spaces where we are called. You wouldn't just stand there idly, waiting for the next move to come along. You wouldn't be the victim, feeling like an accident for being here. You would occupy. You would fill the space and engage it. You would be a part of the story. Even if you feel so small, there's an essential part for you to play.

STEAL THIS PRAYER

Dear God, I need you to show up in the process of rebuilding. I don't want to start over. Do whatever you have to do in my heart to keep me from running from the work. Help me occupy new space.

Chapter Four	# DIG WIDE, DIG DEEP

For as long as I can remember, I've loved the idea of transformation. I am a sucker for all shows that involve a makeover. I love watching people change. I am the person who loves two-week and thirty-day challenges. I want transformation without real, sacrificial change.

During my first month in Atlanta, I picked up a book called *Seven* by Jen Hatmaker. It's a book about sacrifice and learning to live with less. Most people read this book and then decide they are going to take on a challenge. I don't know how to be lukewarm when it comes to challenges, so I pulled out the toughest challenge I could find in the book and started that day. I didn't prepare; I just dug in.

In the book, Jen challenges herself to eat only seven foods for a month. I was enamored with this idea immediately. I picked my seven foods and went to the grocery store. I got kale, though I don't know how to prepare kale. I got sweet potatoes, though I don't know how to make those either. At this point in my life, I wasn't a cook. I only knew how to make eggs and popcorn really. So naturally, eggs and popcorn were two of the seven foods I allowed myself to consume.

"I'm only eating seven foods for a month," I told the barista at the neighborhood coffee shop I stopped at daily. It was a little shop called Taproom, and it was quickly becoming my second home. I told her this like she should care about my well-being or should be amazed at me for practicing such discipline. I think she was none of these things, but she went along with it and asked questions.

"How are the sweet potatoes?" she asked me the next day, and I told her how I tried to make sweet potato toast, but it was actually harder than it looks. My sweet potatoes ended up being raw, but I ate them anyway out of desperation.

"How are the sweet potatoes?" she asked on the third day, and I crumbled and told her I got Wendy's instead.

"I can't do it," I admitedt to her. "It's too hard."

In reality, I had no motive. I had this feeling inside me that I wanted to change something, but I didn't dig deeper than that. I thought hard-boiled eggs would solve something, but I was ultimately stuck until I asked harder questions: What do you really need to change? What is really standing in the way of you being different?

I think being in relationship with God makes asking those questions a little bit harder. A lot of times, God isn't asking us to go to the store and buy hair coloring. He's asking us to change something on the inside. More than that, he's asking us to step away and let him do the work. We, being reluctant humans, want to exercise our right to be fixers. God isn't interested in a story where we get to take all the credit. He doesn't hand us a list of ten simple fixes and then pat us on the back. His change is slower and it's more of a lifelong thing. In a world begging to distract us, God stands in the middle and asks us to follow with a single-minded focus.

None of this appealed to me. I liked quick fixes. I liked

instant results. I wanted to be able to talk loudly about change and how much I loved changing for the better, but I only wanted the change to be as deep as the bottom of a bowl of mashed sweet potatoes. Real change doesn't happen overnight. My friend Ally says real change happens when we reach the end of ourselves. She says that unfortunately people spend a whole lifetime organizing every little detail so they never have to visit that place.

Thirty days into living in Atlanta, all the boxes of hair dye and raw sweet potatoes caught up to me. I was doing everything I thought I needed to do to make Atlanta my home. I was going on coffee dates with basically everyone in the city. I was telling them all my best stories. I was impressing people and then moving on to someone new. Getting coffee with someone for the first time is really easy. You can deep-dive, but you aren't obligated to follow up after that. You know what's hard? Getting coffee with someone who already knows your best stories. Getting coffee with someone after the "get to know you" stage has worn off. That's when the real work begins.

At the time, I rented office space from a guy named Jeff, who is a real powerhouse in the city of Atlanta. He has a way of bringing people who are doing good work together and creating community.

On the day of my quarter-life crisis, Jeff said to me, "You're here. You've been in Atlanta for one month. You've met a lot of people. Now you could keep going on coffee dates with every single person in the city, but it's time for you to start asking yourself the question: Who do I want to see again? You need to take the day off and answer that question for yourself."

Here's what Jeff was basically saying: If you want to have

real relationships, you're going to have to work harder than this. Friendships cannot be sustained in one meeting.

"You could go wide forever," he continued. "But at some point, you're going to have to go deep with people."

I didn't know who I wanted to see again or if I even wanted to bother to see anyone again.

I think back on that day and the advice that Jeff gave and I wonder how he knew to steer me in that direction. I was having a "life crisis," and yet he steered me back toward people. He didn't tell me to eat more spinach. He didn't tell me to go on more walks or read more books. He didn't even say, "Show up before God." He simply asked, "Who do you want to see again?" I think we forget just how important people are to helping us change. We can change on our own, but other people are often the catalysts who push us to the edge of believing we could be someone different when we land.

I didn't take Jeff's advice. Not really. I took half of it. I asked myself the question, "Who do you want to see again?" but I never took the day off. Instead, I went to a midnight showing of *The Fault in Our Stars* with my new friend Nia that evening.

I don't recommend watching this movie if you are in the midst of a twenty-four-hour life crisis. It will not help you. The movie is about two young people with cancer who fall in love. I've never cried harder in a movie theatre before. I can't even call it crying, really. I was full-out grieving for every little thing I'd neglected to cry for in the last seven years. I cried for old boyfriends and failed friendships. I cried for clothes that didn't fit anymore and clothes in the closet that never got worn more than once. I cried for loss and war and politics and soul mates past.

The thing that really gets me about the movie is that the two people falling in love are so different. One of them, Augustus Waters, wants to be remembered forever, on these big, memorable scales. The other, Hazel Grace, is more focused on the present moment because, really, that's all we get.

I think a lot of us are familiar with sitting in the middle of that tension. We want to be seen and known. We want to do big things. But at the end of the day, we really just want to be loved. We want the people at our funerals to know more about us than how impressive we looked on the outside. The thing is, you must allow people to get to know you if you ever want to be anything but impressive to them.

Nia and I sat in the car after the movie, saying nothing for a really long time. My face was puffy beyond recognition, and Nia had no idea in the car that night that I wished I could be someone different. It wasn't this big, overwhelming feeling. It was just this humming in the background of my life that was getting louder and closer. It was the sound of reality announcing its name in the conference call, saying, "I'm here whenever you're ready to see me."

That message—"you need people more than you think"—kept showing up in the days and weeks ahead as I resisted roots in Atlanta. One evening, I was sitting in the corner of Taproom working late. This had become my habit instead of building lasting relationships.

I worked for myself, so all I had to do was create more work if I wanted to close off, shut down, or isolate myself. I didn't want to work at my faith or relationships anymore. This whole "becoming rooted" thing seemed too hard.

I was making small talk with Jonathan, the owner of the coffee shop, that night as he walked around to wipe the tables. It was nearing closing time, and I was one of three people left in the shop.

"You know," he said to me. "I wonder about you sometimes."

"Oh, yeah?" I asked. I was intrigued. I always liked to be that person who sparked wonder in other people. "What do you wonder about?"

I expected some romantic answer that painted me as better than I really was.

"I just wonder about who picks you up from the airport. That's all."

With that statement, he turned on his heels and walked toward the back of the coffee shop. He could see right through me. He could see I was only dipping my toe into the water. I was inviting people in and then hitting the pause button when they asked to get to know me—grabbing my suitcase and heading to the airport for another destination.

I wasn't vulnerable. Not really. I was too afraid to be vulnerable and ask for help, to ask anyone in my life, "Will you pick me up from the airport?"

Jonathan's question came on the heels of my coming back from yet another speaking engagement. This time, I spoke to the international chapter of a sorority at its annual convention in Indianapolis. I really fell in love with this crew. They adopted me in and made me an honorary member of their group for a few days. That was me though; I could fit in anywhere—walk the walk and talk the talk—as long as I had the option of leaving when the honeymoon period wore off.

I stood before a crowd of twelve hundred sorority women

and watched each one of them leave their seat to give me a standing ovation after I spoke. Back in my hotel room, I had this feeling of pride like, "Yes, I matter so much," but I was hit with a sinking feeling of loneliness when I looked at my phone and realized I had no one to celebrate with. Who in my life even knows I'm on this trip to begin with? I was getting so good at leaving, running to somewhere new, that people stopped trying to keep up. I wondered why it wasn't enough for me to share this news with people I loved. I was holding everyone at arm's length. I was saying, *I want you, but I feel like my life is about to get messy, and that? Well, I don't think that's something I want you to see.*

This kept happening though. I kept looking for another chance to leave. To check out. To not have to deal with my own feelings. At one point, I got an email from a reader inviting me to come to her bridal shower in North Carolina. So I went. I spent an entire Saturday driving four hours to the bridal shower of someone I didn't know to surprise her. I spent the day sitting with her bridesmaids and her aunts.

Maybe to all outward appearances this seems like an extravagantly generous way to spend a Saturday. But the truth is, I don't think I went just for the bride's reaction to my actually showing up. I went for my own sake—to spend a day feeling like I was a special guest—and ultimately to leave again, no strings attached.

I was acting like a hurricane, all over the place. I wasn't making lasting friendships; I was plotting the next chance to impress everyone before I found my suitcase at the door.

Along with the bridal showers of strangers, there were dating applications. There were a lot of them. I went on every kind of date. I went on blind dates and Tinder dates. At one point, I was on this app known as "Coffee Meets Bagel." Every day at noon, without fail, a bagel is delivered to you. This bagel is actually a human you might end up making babies with if the sparks fly. In my case, my bagels were men who sometimes had jobs and sometimes had hair.

Rules of the app: You get one metaphorical bagel a day. You determine if you want to talk to the bagel or pass it on to other people—aka, be charitable with your surplus of bagels. You only get one man bagel every twenty-four hours. I still don't know where the coffee enters the equation. I only ever met bagels, no coffee.

Thanks to these dating applications, I went on a parade of bad dates all over Atlanta. I tried to smile and look cute as I and my boys talked about nearly everything—bed bugs, religion, thermostats, what to do if someone ever shows up in your house to kidnap you. One guy took it upon himself to follow every one of my friends on Twitter before the date. I was halfway through an appetizer with another guy when a train went by somewhere in the distance.

"I know that sound," he said to me. "I remember that sound!"

"The sound of the train?"

"That was the same sound Jesus made when he came back!"

"Oh," I said. "I didn't . . . I guess I . . . I guess I just didn't know Jesus was back yet." I kid you not, the guy patted my wrist and said we clearly believed in two different things. It is extremely hard to go back to eating your appetizer when the man across from you is convinced that the second coming has already come and gone. I tried though. My friends still cannot believe I stayed through appetizers, dinner, and dessert with him. I wanted to be kind.

I went around Atlanta gathering an impressive collection of Tinder date horror stories. One date was so boring that I blurted out in the middle of it, "Okay—new topic! Someone breaks into your home in the middle of the night to abduct you. What do you do?"

He stared at me with big eyes, unamused by my trying to shake things up and keep them interesting. That guy never texted me again, and I am thankful.

As I collected dates like playing cards, I knew more dates were never going to fill whatever hole was growing on the inside of me, getting bigger with each guy I decided to never text back.

Let's just start there. I'm used to being a hole filler. I still have hole-filling habits that return from time to time. And trust me, I have tried to fill the holes with everything but a weighty and spiritual God-man. I tried everything I possibly could to not have to let God or people in.

I have a pretty extensive list of everything I tried to fill myself with before I gave up, came to the end of myself:

- dating applications
- gossip
- diets
- restrictions
- plans
- new notebooks
- new friendships

- bigger projects
- more speaking engagements
- guys
- guys who texted back
- French fries (and other forms of potatoes)
- more guys
- workout plans
- *Gilmore Girls*

I say *Gilmore Girls* because that's when I remember it all going downhill. October 1, 2014. I can mark that date on the calendar because it is when *Gilmore Girls* came out on Netflix. I think sometimes Netflix series with a lot of episodes are just a really long and winding distraction to keep us from facing our junk. And that's exactly what Rory and Lorelai helped me do—avoid myself and all the symptoms of depression that were coming on strong like a tidal wave.

I hid behind work. I made excuses to keep me from meeting up with people again. I went to my office space on Friday and Saturday night. I lit a candle and tried to spend time with God. If anyone asked, I was on a pilgrimage, and no one can argue against that. If you want to try to get holier on a Friday night, no one is going to stand in your way.

In reality, I was desperately lonely. I was running on empty, burned out from impressing people but never stopping to be filled up. The Bible would stir nothing in me. I would give up after fifteen minutes. And then I'd retreat to my swivel chair, where I could pretend I was the second sister to Rory, taking my coffee black from Luke while waiting for my mom to come through the door of our favorite coffee joint in Stars Hollow.

That's what I loved about Rory and Lorelai—they were always reliable. You could always count on the coffee being fresh in each episode. They didn't change their plans or become wrecking balls—no, they always managed to stay pretty predictable. They always made you feel welcome, even if from behind a screen. To me, Rory and Lorelai were more reliable than God.

I stopped looking for God in every circumstance because I wouldn't have cared if I could actually find him. I only wanted God if he promised to do what I hoped for. I know that sounds selfish, but I cannot offer you anything but honesty. I think God can handle our broken hearts and broken expectations. He's not afraid of things we're actually thinking about in the here and now. He welcomes our complaints and our sad feelings. Where other people would walk away from us or talk behind our backs, God says, *You miserable little human whom I love, I'm not asking you to get an attitude shift before we hang out.* God doesn't see us as construction zones covered in caution tape, but that's usually how we see ourselves.

––––––––

So I'm going to act as big sister right now and just advise you to avoid doing everything I did if you move somewhere new. Embrace the awkwardness and get comfortable with being uncomfortable. Don't run from it. Be honest with people about the transition and what feels hard. People find honesty to be refreshing. And please, for the love of lovelier things, don't try to charm people with stories about how much you don't like being where you are. That's a way to lose your footing fast. I did this more times than I can count.

"So how are you liking Atlanta?" someone would ask me.

And that was my doorway. That was my chance to say, "It's good. It's a cool place. But do you know what's really cool? The place I came from." I'm in awe of the way we romanticize the things we willingly left behind when the present moment starts testing us.

That's how we build walls high and sturdy. We stop letting people in. We deny people the right to get to know us and demolish the bridge of relationship they are trying to build. We tell them we don't like where we are and we don't desire to be there. It's like trying to make friends with someone when there's a For Sale sign hanging in front of their house. Why bother?

I have a friend in Atlanta who told me that when he first met me at a dinner my roommate hosted, he thought there was something seriously off about me. He said he spent a large chunk of that night trying to figure me out, but ended up concluding I was just hiding behind a lot of achievements. He thought I was completely guarded, and he wondered what stood behind all those walls I'd built for myself.

Yet I want to invite God into this mess. My friend Laura once wrote on Instagram, "God is a perfectly punctual man with a sense of humor." I would add to the quote: "Half the time I think his watch is broken, and I don't think he's all that funny." I like to imagine him coming up beside me as I leave yet another event with arms crossed, mad at myself for reminiscing about the "there" I used to live instead of just learning how to be here. I picture him grabbing my arm like, "Hey, talk to me." And me being a brat, slinking away and trying to ignore him.

I picture myself yelling at him, telling him this was stupid and pointless to move to a new place if I was never going to get good at it. I wasn't leaning into friendships. There was nothing instant about getting involved in a church. I wasn't any less homesick. This was not the plotline in movies I've watched. Television shows neglect the whole six-month period when you feel utterly alone and insignificant while also being "the new girl." There is no funny opening chorus or cute neighbor next door. It's just you burning eggs in the kitchen. You FaceTiming friends who are hundreds of miles away. You reading your Bible and feeling that because you don't feel God, he must not be here.

I picture God stopping me. He remains completely calm. He looks at me like, *Really? You really want to cause this scene?* He reminds me of a story that's happened to him before. It was the time he promised an entire people group a land flowing with milk and honey, but there was one stipulation: they had to get there. They had to take that long road through a million other lands before they got to their own Promised Land. And when they were feeling hungry on the journey, he rained down bread for them to eat.

Bread from the sky is a pretty impressive feat, and I'm never one to turn down carbs, but the people hate this. They can't get over how much they hate this act of God. They want meat. They want something else. God handles them in their completely bratty ways and continues to provide for them. When they eventually get to that Promised Land, God hands them shovels and tells them that getting food will look a little bit different now. They will have to dig for it. They will have to produce it. And the people, because they're basic humans like you and me, get upset again. Because they've gotten used to the flying bread. They don't want a new level of responsibility. They don't want things to change. They don't want to feel less comfortable than they were yesterday.

The moral of the story is this: God doesn't stop providing. He's constant in the provision, whether we see it or not. It's just that sometimes he starts providing differently, depending on what we need for the moment. And we don't like that. We reject that whole story because we like it when things stay the same. This life is not about staying the same—unless you want to die inside. I picture God looking at me sternly, but with a deep love in his eyes, as he tells me, *Stop whining about the flying bread. If you're always relying on my old provision, you'll never see what I'm doing for you right now. Grab the shovel, and I'll show you how to dig deep.*

STEAL THIS PRAYER

Dear God, it is so much easier to go wide. I want to run into the spotlight. I want the applause. I want to be affirmed and I want approval. Help me to want something better than this. Show me a life that is deeper than this.

Chapter Five	# WALK IN THE VALLEY

> We are not made for the mountains, for sunrises, or for the other beautiful attractions in life—those are simply intended to be moments of inspiration. We are made for the valley and the ordinary things of life, and that is where we have to prove our stamina and strength.
>
> **Oswald Chambers, *My Utmost for His Highest***

"Can I come home yet?" I ask her.

We are standing in the middle of a crowded church lobby. I am in Connecticut for the first time since moving to Atlanta. I am talking to Carol, someone who has been a spiritual mentor to me for the last few years. She's someone who mapped out my entire first book with me and gave me her home for days on end when I needed a writing retreat. I've slept on her couch while she and her husband have gone on date nights and brought me home ice cream like I'm their child.

"It's been six months and I don't feel like anything is happening," I tell her.

Translation: my expectations have been popped. The vision in my head of what I thought a new city would look like has not come to fruition, and I would like to give up now.

"No," she says matter-of-factly. "You're in the valley."

I've never been able to understand why Christians talk about "the valley" so much. If you stick around church long enough, you'll start hearing it trickle into everyday speech. We talk about the valley like we're all on some pilgrimage, hauling backpacks across dry land for years before we see any sight of water. I've learned no one ever talks about the valley like it's a good thing. Just the opposite—everyone dreads the valley. So when I write *valley*, I really just mean a place in your faith or your life where you feel like nothing is moving and nothing good is happening.

"You're in the valley," she repeats to me again, as if I didn't hear her say it the first time. "You've experienced a lot of high highs and a lot of low lows in the last few years. God wants to teach you how to walk in the everyday of life."

Another translation: no, you can't come home. Pop the bubble in your mind causing you to believe everything in life is meant to be rhythmic and romantic. You are not Meg Ryan. This is not a repeat of *You've Got Mail*. This is your life. And you need to learn how to live inside it instead of always thinking leaving is going to fix the reasons you don't want to stay.

When everything was exciting and new, I was happy to be in Atlanta. I liked exciting. I liked new. But eventually things stop being cool and we are left with everyday life. We are left with every moment that isn't worth documenting or blasting all over social media.

"You're in the valley." This is her third time saying it. "Welcome to it."

She touches my shoulder as if she's welcoming me to a club she's been in for years. I feel like a Girl Scout now who's just been initiated and given a bare Brownie sash. I want all the badges already, but I've done none of the work.

I do all the normal things when I fly home that first time. I go to a baby shower for a friend. I hang out at a diner with people I love. I eat popcorn and binge-watch episodes of *General Hospital* with my mom. I even make a fool of myself sitting in front of a guy I used to date, telling him I want to try again. I am not sure I really want to try again, but I am ravenous for the familiar. At this point, I would be willing to take back any boyfriend from my past if he requested I just come home. I am looking for something to tether me back to this place where I am comfortable. I will light this plane ticket on fire with a blowtorch if anyone in the vicinity of my childhood zip code tells me they can't live without me and I need to stay.

The guy sitting with me in the coffee shop rejects me. He doesn't want to play this game with me. I think I am acting sincere, but I am really just being pathetic. It hurts to be home because I look around and realize everyone is doing just fine. Church is still happening on Sunday. People are still falling in love. Guys I dated are moving on. It's painful to realize the world doesn't revolve around you and people go on living once you leave.

I spend the rest of my time at home in Connecticut plowing through the Bible, searching for every reference to a valley I can find. I'm largely motivated by knowledge, so if you tell me I'm standing in a valley, I am going to learn everything I possibly can about that valley.

Turns out, valleys are depressing places in the Bible, too,

when we first look at them. Look a little closer though. Something happens in the valley. Something really beautiful and necessary happens in the valley. But really, this is most of my relationship with God. I see some dismal outcome and God is constantly pushing me to look closer and see something different.

I just want the instant solutions. I want the clarity. I want God to pluck me out of this time of waiting, give me all the answers I'm asking for, and then send me on my way to my next adventure.

And so I tell him, "Pluck me out of this time of waiting, give me all the answers I am asking for, and then send me on my way to my next adventure, God. Let's do this thing!"

But no. He just leads me to Leviticus. Where there is plenty of valley stuff. Like God is sending me to my room, I get sent to the confines of Leviticus. And Leviticus is not the book of the Bible you read when you want to be affirmed.

I begin sitting with the Israelites, and let me tell you, the Israelites are real bundles of fun when it comes to this waiting stuff. They're never happy. They're always complaining. There's always something bad happening to an Israelite. Imagine every troll you've ever encountered on Facebook paired with the people you're forced to unfollow because they get political about everything in the world. Band these two populations into a people group and you've basically got the Israelites.

In the Old Testament, the Israelites escape Egypt and end up at the foot of Mount Sinai. Scholars call this the "Wilderness of Sinai." A real eccentric website from 1998 (complete with flashing GIFs) tells me they camped at the foot of Sinai for eleven months and five days. The text says they spent those months resting, teaching, building, and meeting with God face-to-face.

This sounds beautiful in theory, but we often don't realize the sweetness of something until it is out of our hands. I bet I would say to God, "No way. Absolutely no way will I spend a year resting and hanging out. I need to be doing. I need to be going. I need chaos to add order to my life."

We'd label those Israelites as lazy today. We would say they were making no progress. We are so obsessed with the hustle and the grind that we don't know how to stop and wait on God.

I think about Moses, the guy in charge of leading those Israelites, and how he climbed up the mountain of Sinai to meet with God. He stayed there for forty days and forty nights. While Moses is up there, chaos erupts on the ground. This whole time, Moses has been leading the people alongside his brother Aaron. They were a team. You'd think it was a perfectly good idea to leave Aaron in charge while Moses went up the mountain.

Moses is probably gone for less than a day before the Israelites go stir-crazy and want a new god. They can't wait. They decide they're going to make their own god, and they settle on a golden calf to worship. And where is Aaron in the chaos? He's just casually welding a cow for them. He goes from serving God to making another god for the restless, angry people.

We look at this and think we would never do something so dumb. But you can replace the word *cow* with anything we find in everyday life that we think could fill us more than God could. I think I would be a front-runner in worshiping that gold-glinted cow. I would definitely be dancing around the cow in the hope that the cow would affirm me and make me feel alive. In a lot of ways, I understand why Aaron made that god for the people. Sometimes you just want to worship something you can touch— something right in front of you that feels real.

Moses comes off the mountaintop and has to face all of this crap. There's not a better word for it than that—it's just pure crap that Moses has to deal with with these people. By this time, the people have created golden cow T-shirts, posters, and trinkets. If I'd been Moses, I would have wanted to be done. I would have been angry over the fact that I'd just had this perfect time and communion with God and then was forced to walk down the mountain and go back to reality. Reality is the tough stuff. It's people dancing around a cow made out of gold and thinking it's good enough. Reality is what happens when we make ourselves come back to earth instead of running.

I think we all want to run sometimes. We want to run because it feels too hard to stay in these places where we aren't sure of what's coming next. And we all get a little stir-crazy for a god who will finally get us some answers.

I personally think there should be a national holiday called "I'm Really Unsure about Life Day," when we can cheer one another on for being so uncertain about what's happening. I'm aware that some people already celebrate this holiday regularly, but we could have a parade with different floats. We could wear crowns and sashes. We would turn all of this "valley living" into a festivity. We could rejoice because that's what faith tells us to do—rejoice, even when you're not sure. I'm learning the value of singing, even when I don't know the tune.

Walk, even when you don't know where to step next. Just keep walking and you'll see what I saw: the valley is full. When I think I am on a solo quest, I realize the valley is full of travelers. Some are plowing full steam ahead. Others are tired and have stopped walking. Oswald Chambers writes, "God gives us a vision, and then He takes us down to the valley to batter us into the shape of that vision. It is in the valley that so many of us faint and give way."[1]

_____

"Choosing to stay in Charleston is the hardest thing ever," my friend Ashley texted me recently. "There are no hugs here. I cry all the time, and this is the loneliest I have ever been."

She moved to Charleston on a whim because she thought it was the destination. Like me, she thought she would arrive and everything would be easy after that. Two months in, she was wrong—even though from the looks of her life online, she is happy in her new place.

"I feel like an empty, fragile shell—not an actual person. But I've loved Charleston my whole life. I thought God wanted me here, and I hope I wasn't wrong. I can't let Charleston be the place where I decided to give up on myself."

What do you text to a friend when they've spilled their whole heart out to you like coffee all over a white shirt? What do you say to soak up their pain and wring it out?

My thumbs hovered over the screen before I typed the words I know by heart. "Oh, girl. You're in the valley."

Send. I paused. I kept typing.

"Welcome to it."

I cannot tell her what will happen next. I cannot whip out the map and show her the peaks she will experience and the lower-than-she-thought-possible places she may go in the next few months. To be a good friend, I tell her to keep walking. I tell her to keep her head up.

_____

1. Oswald Chambers, *My Utmost for His Highest* (New York: Dodd, Mead, 1935), July 6.

I tell her to hit her knees and keep hitting her knees to the floor. Dig prayers from the inside of your belly and keep digging until you find the words to give God. Don't worry if they are scrappy, tired, or feel fake. God wants every prayer you've got— every decent, ugly, uncivilized prayer inside of you. He loves them unscripted and honest.

I pray one of those scrappy prayers when I fly back to Atlanta from visiting Connecticut. I listened to Carol telling me I needed to go back and figure out how to walk in the valley. Shortly after flying back, I head to a retreat center in northern Georgia for a speaking engagement.

This is a retreat center I'd been going to for years. It's the same women's conference, and I speak at it annually, but it has become so much more to me than a chance to get on a stage and talk to a room filled with more than two hundred women. This place, in the hills of northern Georgia, has become—for better or worse—my gauge with God. I think we all might have these places. They are spots we go to where we know the noise will be less and the pressures of everyday life will slip off our shoulders for a little while. When the noise stops, and the pressure is off, I can gauge where I'm really at. It's a point where I can stop, hit pause, and look for that little blue spot on the map that reads "You Are Here."

My car rolls past the front gate. I know the way by heart as I drive up the hill and park in the back of the building at the top of the hill. At the door to the room where I will be staying all week, I wheel my little red suitcase in and leave it parked by the bed. I survey the bedroom. There's a bright blue bedspread and chicken decor. So much chicken decor all over the room. I put my keys beside a chicken lamp and open the door to the closet. Like I said, I've been here before so I know that when I open the closet, the walls will be filled with other people's messages. This retreat center is used throughout the year as a place to come when your marriage is about to break. Estranged couples stay in the very room I'm staying in, and when the retreat is over, they walk into the closet and write down whatever God has done. A lot of people are gauging where they're at with God in this place.

I walk into the bathroom and stop in front of the tub. I've never seen a tub so massive and deep. Some people find God most in a church with stained-glass windows, but me and God— we've got a thing for tubs.

The tub is inviting me, beckoning, "Come inside. Have a seat."

I give in to the tub's request and step inside. I sit down. I kick the soles of my Nike pumps against the porcelain knobs and lie back. I close my eyes. I just stay in that tub for a really long time. I don't reach for my phone.

I usually have a lot of things to say to God because I am a person who rarely lacks words. But here I am, speechless. Maybe you've been in my spot before. It's the moment when you had really high expectations for something and it just didn't work out like you thought it would. You prayed a lot of prayers. You did your best, but it feels like God has other plans and maybe you weren't prepared for that. I am learning God doesn't bring us places to meet our expectations. For him, it's a lot more about the transformation. He loves who we are, but he will never pass up on the chance to use life events to make us better.

I feel like I am waiting for God in this tub. Waiting in the way you wait for a text from someone you like too much—expectantly, but with a self-deprecating fear that they aren't interested in you. It's crazy to me how I can spend so much of my life trying to please God and still think he doesn't want me at the end of the day.

I start to pick at the polish on my nails. Flecks of red fall off and all around me into the tub. I wonder if I should say something, start the conversation with, "Hey, I miss you. Where have you been? I feel like you're not around anymore, even though everyone keeps saying your name."

I couldn't lie to people anymore and claim that God and I were "doing good." I was so sick of saying we were good when really it felt like divorce court every time I sat down with my Bible. In my reality, we were estranged. We were barely speaking. I became like a ghost in my own faith life. I knew all the motions, but I wasn't really there. I was lying to everyone about where God and I were on the map. If you're lying about where you are, people can't find you.

I mumble into the depths of the tub. "I don't know if I heard you wrong about coming to Atlanta. Or maybe I didn't hear you at all. Maybe I just heard my own voice."

The words of my prayer sound like a precursor to a breakup.

"I can't do this any longer though," I say. "I mean, I can't fake this. I can't get up onstage and talk about you. I can't tell people about you if you're not real. I need you to be real or I can't keep going."

I stay a little longer in the tub. I wait.

"If you are real, than be real," I whisper in a pleading voice, losing hope that I will get a response.

"Be real, be real, be real."

Two weeks after this prayer, the fight to become something better than what I was would begin.

STEAL THIS PRAYER

Dear God, I am laying down my armor and I am choosing not to run from what's next. I want momentum, but I know you work in the slow progress and in the times when I think you aren't even here. Make me brave enough to live without the things that slow me down. Change me. Break me. Refine me. I want to become who I was made to be.

Chapter Six | SAY YES IN THE DARK

I take a small white pill every other day with a swig of water. The pill with the green line around the capsule is a reminder to me that November 18, 2014, happened. There are just days that show up on the calendar as an unassuming weekday and then change everything about your life.

The first half of November 18 was pretty normal. I went to work at my office space in Atlanta. I sat in a meeting. I filmed a short video for a company. I worked at my desk, trying to focus on my writing, but my mind wouldn't sit still. I walked into the conference room where my friend Kim was working and asked her to pray for me.

"My mind doesn't do well when I don't have a lot on my plate," I told her. "I really don't like asking for prayer, but I feel like I can't keep this to myself today."

Kim began praying. I sat across from her, fidgeting with my hands and trying to listen and believe the words coming out of her mouth. When she says amen, my head lifts. She starts talking about something, though I can't really remember what, because all I can recall in that moment is a sharp pain. This sharp, physical pain that began at the top of my head and cascaded down across my body. It felt like a power outage, like all the systems were going down, and all of a sudden, I couldn't move. I couldn't think. There was a mental snap inside my brain, and suddenly I was helpless. My mind was paranoid and darting back and forth. I felt sick. I got up from the chair and told Kim I didn't feel well. I needed to go home.

I drove home. It was 4 p.m. I curled up in my bed and wrote in my journal, "What is happening?" I still don't have adequate words to describe what it felt like. The best I can say is that I felt completely paralyzed by fear.

There was sharp paranoia. I felt like my brain was being attacked. I didn't leave my bed that day. I kept praying to God that this feeling would subside soon. Maybe it was the food I ate. I prayed it was just a bad reaction to gluten or something. I fell asleep shaking somewhere around 8 p.m. The notebook lay open beside me with the words, "What is wrong with me?" scribbled in Sharpie across the page.

The next morning, I woke up unable to get out of bed. A thick and heavy paralysis sat on top of me like an extra layer of blankets. It took me a half hour to get up and get dressed. I had to go to Baltimore that morning for a speaking engagement and there was no way I could cancel with such short notice.

It was literally zero degrees in Baltimore when I got there. I was due to speak the next morning, so the professor from the community college where I would be giving my talk picked me up from the airport and dropped me off at the hotel. I remember the carpet of my hotel room best out of anything else about that trip because I laid there, head in the carpet, for hours upon arrival. I kept praying for clarity, asking for God to help, begging to know what was happening inside my brain. I felt like God was being quiet.

I didn't sleep that night. I kept tossing back and forth,

feeling like there was a war going on in my mind and I was just a confused civilian caught in the mess. I got up and spoke the following morning at 8 a.m. I kept whispering to myself, "Just hold yourself together. Just keep it together."

A few hours later, I was back at the airport with four hours to spare. I darted through the Baltimore airport looking for a gate that wasn't being occupied. I curled up in a ball, using the hard plastic airport seats as a makeshift bed. I sent a text to friends in Connecticut, friends I knew would pray for me: "I don't know what's going on. I can't shake this fear. Please pray."

I went back and forth between my makeshift bed and the restroom, dry heaving into the toilet. I had no idea that this was the beginning of the storm.

————————

I'm no stranger to depression. I had gone through depression once before, when I was living in New York City four years earlier. I didn't know the statistics and just assumed depression was like the chicken pox: once you deal with it, that's it, never again. In reality, they say those who have suffered with depression once are 80 percent likely to go for round two.

I ignored whatever warning signs were encroaching around me as it led up to November 18. I refused to see a therapist, even though my friend Eryn thought it might help me. I isolated myself. I stopped being honest. I pulled back from relationships. All of the classic symptoms were there, but I tried to fly under the radar. I should have seen the crash coming from miles away. If only I could have just mapped the storm before it hit.

And so began a long stretch of looking for answers, figuring out how I went from being one of the most driven people to someone who could barely perform basic tasks. I was flying and driving back and forth between Atlanta and Connecticut. I couldn't work. I couldn't sleep. I was plagued by nightmares, waking up too afraid to lie back down.

Doctors couldn't explain it. The best answer I got was that it would take six to twelve months of intense rehabilitation therapy to get me back to a "normal" functioning state. I don't know how you even use the word *normal* in this case. What did life look like before this? What would I actually be going back to? At one point, a doctor prescribed me with a benzodiapamine as a temporary solution—"a way to calm you down." I was swallowing the pills in the hope I could just claw myself back to reality. I didn't know benzos will calm you down at first, but the anxiety will build back up and spike back harder than it was before once the drug wears off. When I would crash, Depression and Anxiety would scoop me up again and feed me another batch of panic attacks.

I learned pretty quickly that Depression and Anxiety make a fantastic team. I don't want to give them that much credit, but they work really well together. A lot of people say Depression and Anxiety are sisters to one another. You are usually diagnosed with both of them at the same time. Together, they try to manipulate their master plan to keep you in place.

Depression says to you, "Hey, I want you to feel low. I want you to hate getting out of bed. I want you to have one longing—to go back to sleep." Depression is interested in your past; it obsesses over it. It wants you to be so fixated on things that have already happened that you get stuck there. You can't release whatever is holding you back and so you sink into it. Depression repeats, "Remember how good you used to have it? Remember how happy you used to be? Too bad you are alone now. Too bad you're stuck with me." It convinces you that you're alone. You are needy. You are weak. You should just give up.

At some point, Anxiety joins in on the taunting. Anxiety doesn't really care about your past because it would rather make you crazy worrying about what's going to happen next. Anxiety has an anthem that tells you, "Bad stuff is on the horizon. You are going to ruin relationships. You are going to lose that job. You won't be able to pay the bills." Anxiety makes up all these phantom pains and adds them to your story so you can't figure out what is real and what is just worry.

Together that team—Anxiety and Depression—took turns hanging out with me. It felt like a custody battle between the two of them, both fighting for whatever was left of my brain. I'd get these short glimpses of perspective toward the end of the day where everything felt clear and felt right to me. I didn't feel anxious. I didn't feel sad. It felt like the moment someone pulls you out of a pool after you've been drowning. They wrap you in a towel and you are safe. You are held. You are okay.

In those moments when it felt like the darkness wasn't going to win, I'd go to my computer and open a document I titled "Coming Out of the Woods." I would write the day and the time. I'd write myself a little note, a little reminder that I wasn't gone. This small ounce of hope rose up in me that maybe it was over. Maybe the darkness would flee this time. I would go to sleep so hopeful, but then wake back up in that fog. It's a fog I still can't fully articulate, but it feels like you're trapped in a small box with no windows and no doors. It feels like the space is getting smaller and like no one knows you're stuck in there so there's no point in hoping they'll come back with the key.

I lost ten pounds. I stopped being able to digest the world

around me—television shows would trigger a breakdown and movies would send me into a tailspin in my brain. I would sit on my bed for hours at a time and just stare at the wall, unable to count or gather how much time had gone by.

The nights were the worst. For the first month of the depression, I had night terrors nearly every evening that would last from midnight to 3 or 4 a.m. Eventually, around 4 a.m., I'd pick my body up from my bed, wrap myself in a blanket, and go sit with my Bible, sometimes not even opening it.

The depression held strong ground for the next two months as I volleyed back and forth between Atlanta and Connecticut. I wasn't staying put. I was packing a bag and leaving more ferociously than ever in the hope that changes in geography could heal me. For a stretch of time in Atlanta, it got to the point where we couldn't avoid the conversation about long-term medication options any longer.

One morning, one of my friends drove me to a clinic in Atlanta. She droppedme off and told me she'd be back to pick me up. I wasn't wearing any makeup on my face at this point. My hair wasn't done. All of the daily tasks of grooming seemed trivial and exhausting to me.

I was summoned into a room, and I sat across from a nurse, who was thin in stature and spoke broken English. He asked me all the preliminary questions that get asked before they let you in to see the doctor.

"Are you having trouble sleeping? Are you self-medicating in any way? Do you have thoughts of harming yourself? Do you have thoughts of harming other people?"

I looked around the sterile office and wondered how I'd gotten there. I tucked my head against the wall, trying to keep my knees from shaking violently.

The man paused in the middle of one of his questions. Our eyes locked, and I could tell he saw how hollowed out I felt in that moment. He put his pen down.

"Are you a Christian?" he asked me. His tone of voice was lower, as if we were talking in secret now.

"I am," I said back to him.

"I'm not supposed to ask that here," he said. "But I just need to tell you that the devil is rejoicing right now, and we will not let him have you."

A moment passed. Our eyes stayed locked. I know he saw a tear dribble down my cheek. He went back to scribbling notes and acting as if he hadn't just given me a secret message. He got up abruptly, shook my hand, and exited the room, saying, "The doctor will be with you shortly."

In that office, I felt like Moses at the point when the Amalekites came to fight the Israelites. The battle was hard. It seemed nearly impossible. Moses discovered that when his arms were raised toward the sky, toward God, then they began to win. When he dropped his arms to his side, things shifted and they started to lose the battle. When his hands began to get tired, Moses's friends came around him and held his arms up for him. They kept him steady. They did this until the battle was won.

Here was a man with broken English in the middle of a doctor's office I'd never been to before, taking my arms and holding them up for me. He didn't need to. It wasn't his job to keep me strong in this fight, but he took on the role. Maybe he has been there before. Maybe he has fought the same war.

Regardless, I felt a little stronger. I felt like I could hold my arms up a little longer until the next person came along to help me keep going.

When you get pressed into the dark, you figure out what you really think about God. You figure out if what you said you believed about God is actually true and whether you will say yes or no to whatever is coming up ahead.

I think at some points throughout this depression that maybe I was praying the wrong prayers. Maybe the prayer isn't, "God, take this away from me." Maybe it's, "God, help me move through this." Avoiding something and moving through something are two very different things.

Maybe that meant I would get a little beat up in the process. I would take some hits. Maybe life isn't about avoiding the bruises, it's about collecting the scars to prove we showed up for it. We think darkness like this could only be a punishment, but maybe it's the start of building something new. I know beautiful things are born out of the dark all the time.

Tim Keller writes about the darkness, "Like fire working on gold, suffering can destroy some things within us and can purify and strengthen other things . . . There is no way to know who you really are until you're tested."[1]

I learn that the building of trust happens in the dark. It happens when we choose not to hide but to charge toward the stuff that scares us most. We figure out what we are holding tightly to, what truly matters, and what we must release to get to the other side safe and sane.

1. Keller, *Walking with God through Pain and Suffering*, 234.

When I say yes to God, I'm saying, "Yes, I will go with you into the dark. I'll take the battles and I'll take the bruises." It's easy to say yes when life is good, the money is coming in, our health is great, and things seem to be working in our favor. But do we say yes in the dark? What is good enough, real enough, strong enough for us that, when everything else fails us, we will still say yes in the dark?

STEAL THIS PRAYER

Dear God, I believe you are doing something in the times when everything feels dark all around me. When I cannot see, teach me to trust you have my next step. Adjust my eyes to see in the dark. Bring me through the hard stuff so I can reach my hand back and help someone else. Help me come out of the woods so I can be a light to others who need it most.

82

| *Chapter* | **STAY IN THE** |
| *Seven* | **WAITING ROOM** |

The depression held strong ground through November and December and into January. I kept going between Atlanta and Connecticut like someone looking for sanctuary.

In Connecticut, women from the church I'd gone to before moving away assembled forces. They came up with a plan to keep me surrounded and to help me recover. They said if I came back, they would help me fight this. It would be much easier to fight the battles standing in one place.

I remember getting on Skype one evening while in Atlanta with one of the women. Her husband joined her on the call. They said very honestly to me that they thought I needed to stop going back and forth and just come back to Connecticut to get stronger. There was a snowstorm coming. I wasn't well. I needed to be surrounded and not isolated. My roots weren't deep enough in Atlanta for me to do this on my own.

Over Skype, I booked a plane ticket for the next day. I slept at my friend's house that night. I lay in bed until I heard her footsteps outside the door the next morning, getting ready to take me to the airport. I pulled a sweater over my head and rolled my suitcase into the hallway. We stopped to eat biscuits that morning. Even though I wasn't walking into anything beautiful when I stepped off the plane, I love how special she made the morning for me. We stopped at the tattoo parlor on the way to the airport because when you're young and in your twenties, you think every step toward bravery should be permanently marked on your body with a needle.

She held my head in her lap and squeezed my hand tight as the tattoo artist inked the letters into the skin of my ribs. First the S, then the T. Next the A and then the Y. The word STAY danced along my rib cage in small, capital letters.

It's ironic to get the word *stay* permanently put on your body right before you board a plane to leave again. While I wasn't exactly embracing a geographic location at the time, I needed a bigger reminder when I chose that word *stay*: stay in the fight. I needed to stay in the struggle. Stay in the wrestling and tumbling with God.

I want to be really careful with this one. For years, my anthem has been "stay." Stay where you are. Stay rooted. Be right where your feet are. That's all well and beautiful, but I don't want to put the message out there that we should stay in toxic situations where our health, faith, and well-being are being compromised. I like to imagine this message of "staying" is synced with the idea that we don't just walk away and call it quits when stuff gets hard. Life is hard. Life will deal us some tough blows. The hard stuff produces character, and I know I could always stand to have more character. So I stay. I want to believe we are capable of staying when the world would otherwise be tempted to pack a suitcase and leave.

_____

That first night back in Connecticut, I meet up with a woman named Nancy, who has the plan for me. She has made it so I will always be occupied and never alone. I think this is incredibly crucial for people who are struggling with depression or other kinds of mental illnesses. The illness wants to isolate you. It wants you to stay in bed. It wants you to spend days on end by yourself so it can whisper to you an identity that isn't yours. The only way to combat that voice? Reach out for help. It's okay to say, "I'm not okay."

We talked out the plan over pizza. I could barely eat anything.

"You know, I would have never guessed anything was wrong," she said to me at one point. "From the looks of social media, it seemed like you were doing just fine."

I thought back over the last few months and how much I'd used social media as a highlight reel for the good things happening to me in a new city. There were a lot of them. Maybe I wasn't doing any heavy-duty work to plant roots, but I'd still met a lot of beautiful people and still had moments that felt worth highlighting. I realize now the dangers of social media in that respect. It's incredibly easy to fool the world into thinking you are happy, surrounded, and doing okay. It's no surprise that the real story isn't usually on social media. We claim to want it, but we also know we don't show up to social media for people's messes. We come for the curation. We come for the eloquent copy and the cute pictures. We come to be amused and receive what is the equivalent of a side hug on the internet.

When you start reaching out, you learn the real story. You see how awful someone's day has been or you get to join them in celebrating something new. You no longer participate in their story through a bird's-eye view. You are in the story. You are real to the story. All the things we build, all the things we think are important about a platform, just don't matter. Followers don't matter. Influence doesn't matter. When the darkness hits, you realize there's a small pocket of people who will meet you at a pizza parlor and help you plot your survival strategy through the storm.

"You know you're going to have to pick at some point," she said to me when we were finishing up the meal. "You'll have to pick a place to make your home. If you never build a home, you'll always be a visitor."

The next month was a fight. My mother and I fought and cried a lot during this time. More crying than there was fighting, but I think we were just so frustrated that this situation couldn't mend itself. You're poring over books, saying prayers, asking God to do a miracle, but the depression is debilitating and it's real, day after day. The tiny light in the tunnel during this is that my mother now sees depression for what it is. Up until this, I think we both thought depression was something that made you sad but maybe to call it suffering was a stretch. As we walked through this pain, we learned we can't help but suffer when someone we love is crushed by despair. We can't help do anything but gather up the pieces of the day and extend them to God and say, "Here, you try to do something with this."

It is lonely. It is hard. No matter what, we kept talking about it.

During this time, I tried to see what God says about the waiting period. About the "in between" that so many of us know by heart. In between cities. In between relationships. In between answers.

There's a story in Jeremiah that I think details it best. In the twenty-ninth chapter, God uses the prophet Jeremiah to write a letter to the Israelites. The Israelites are haywire at this point. They are building their own gods, worshiping kings, making a mess out of humanity. So God basically sends them to a big ole timeout (read, exile) in a place called Babylon. We'd say these people in Babylon were stuck "in between." They were at a crossing in the road between "I thought God's promises were credible and good" and "we're still in the process of getting to those promises." Translation: waiting.

I think waiting is misunderstood a lot of the time. We take this concept of waiting and shove it into the corner like a reject. We misunderstand waiting because we handle it on a daily basis. We wait on the trivial, the mundane, and the sacred, but somehow we still use the same word for all of it. Our world wants to say waiting for things doesn't matter, that you should just go out there and seize what you want.

Waiting is divine. It's this mysterious stretch of time when things seem quiet but God isn't finished yet. We may not hear him talking loudly or be able to call the next play, but the waiting produces grit in us. And grit is absolutely necessary to survive in this world.

I'm sure the anxiety in the hearts of the Israelites distorted the truth about their present moment. I wonder how many times they had to remind themselves not to rest in their own feelings more than they sought after the plans of God.

In the story, God goes on to say that after they live for seventy years in Babylon, he will fulfill his promise to his people:

he will lead them out of exile; he will give them hope and a future. That's where Jeremiah 29:11, the verse we all know from graduation greeting cards, comes in.

But I think we get that verse wrong. I think sometimes we skip right into the promise and forget the big, fat, God-ordained period of waiting these people were faced with. They had to endure the process of waiting before they got the promise.

God doesn't tell the people to sit on their hands and grumble. He doesn't tell them to whine or complain or go rant on Facebook. We think of waiting as a passive, idle thing, but God is really saying, "Make no mistake, there are things you need to do in this waiting period."

God doesn't tell the people of Israel to run away. Just the opposite: *The Message* version of Jeremiah 29:5 reads, "Build houses and make yourselves at home." I translate his advice as, "Get a little comfortable because you're not camping out right now. This won't be instant so you better unpack your suitcases." Running won't help. Distractions only prolong the inevitable.

I woke up one morning in the bed of my childhood home with a searing pain in my right eye. I tried to ignore it. I changed contacts. I realized the ache was getting worse, so I called my eye doctor to see if I could make a last-minute appointment.

An hour later, I found myself sitting in the examination chair at the eye doctor while he quickly prescribed medicine for what turned out to be a corneal ulcer.

"Thankfully you came in right when you did," he told me. "Any later and we might have had to do a corneal transplant."

Turns out, you can get a corneal ulcer from too many tears.

Go figure. He went on to say we'd monitor my eye for the next twenty-four hours. If it didn't get any better, we'd look into surgery. He prescribed me to not wear my contacts, use medicine every two hours, and not expose my eye to too much light. Basically, he told me to lie quietly in a dark room—this is not the best medicine for a person who is already depressed.

I was hesitant to talk about all of this because it's not pretty, and for lack of a better word, it's really depressing. But I can't deny that we should be talking about mental illness more. It matters that we talk about it. That we get real and honest with one another. We have to be okay with telling someone else, "I'm not okay," if we ever want to make progress or stay here for what we were made for. It's easy to be ashamed of the fog, the sickness, the illness. *But what if we broke the shame with words? What if we dismantled the stigma by figuring out how to hold up the arms of others?* So here's a baby step: Please talk about the fog. Please talk about the emptiness. Please don't let yourself stand in the mess alone, so much so that you cave inward and hoist up a white flag without anyone ever knowing you were dying inside.

Those next few days were a new kind of dark as I lay in bed and applied medicine to my eye every two hours. I felt completely numb and defeated, not sure if I could do anything more.

At this point, I'd gone to church services, tried new habits, saw new doctors—whatever people proposed to me. One of my friends offered to drive me two states over to meet with a woman who could take me through a healing process. I agreed to go, and we ended up meeting her in a church, where she invited me to close my eyes, placed her hand on my head, and led me through a forty-five-minute process of forgiving old boyfriends.

When it was over, she told me I would feel better now, but nothing really changed.

I was doing everything I could, hoping every step forward would be an offering that might work to make me better. I lay in bed with a hot towel over my eye and thought about those Israelites again, the ones stuck in Babylon. They had to have had those moments too. Those moments when you want to scream and say, "I am doing everything I can, but I keep getting kicked down! I want to see you move instead, God!"

They said in the Beatitudes that some of us could see God. Blind in one eye and wearing a pirate's patch to avoid getting dizzy, I was so completely helpless at this point, but I was slowly beginning to see things more clearly than ever before.

If you let people in and then keep letting people in, you will see God. If you stay on watch for God—shift your eyes off the problem for five minutes—you will start to see him move around the board like a skilled chess player. You will see him move in a way you didn't think was possible. I saw God every time my mom curled into bed with me at night and held me to stop the violent shaking that ensued throughout the night, every time she made me a cup of tea and stayed up with me when I was too afraid to go to sleep.

I saw God when my friends held my hand for long stretches of time and only let go when I said I was okay. When they woke up at four in the morning to talk on the phone with me and read verses out loud. I saw him in the days when the person beside me knew I didn't feel like talking and that was perfectly okay. They sat with me anyway. Their presence was God in the flesh. In the darkness—in the stuff you don't think you can survive—God sends angels in the form of human beings. Yes, God is still recruiting angels for his mission, but if we never had the heartbreak, we may have never known they were here.

Even though the depression broke my heart, I began to make peace with it. I began to realize that maybe I'd never be healed and maybe that wasn't the point. I got to the point that I was able to say, "God, even if you don't heal me, I will still tell people you are good." For the first time in my life, I knew it. I felt it deeper than anything I'd ever felt before. I was seeing God at work, and it was remarkable.

"This is situational," my mom keeps reminding me. "This is where you are for the moment, but this is not your whole story."

She holds me and she doesn't call me crazy. They all keep holding me and they never call me crazy. They ride out the fog with me. And they stand with me when the fog gets worse and we have to try a different route—the hospital.

When you get to the hospital, you start thinking to yourself, *Shouldn't someone else be standing in my shoes?*

You feel like you're watching a movie in which you're the disheveled character no one can fix. You know your life would never be a movie, because this thing has been going on for months now. This thing isn't resolving itself in two hours.

At the hospital, they lead you down a hallway and you're asked to put all your possessions into a bag. They take the bag from you and lead you into a small room where they close the door and leave you there. The only thing in the room is a chair and a bed. You lie on the bed and the most peace you've felt in a while swarms in all around you. You feel safe now. Maybe you won't have to fight anymore. Maybe you can stay in this bed forever and eventually people will forget about you. It could be over soon.

During these days, it's the closest you've ever come to considering suicide. The idea never gets too deep or elaborate, but you get it now. You understand why some people think it would be easier to die than to feel like your mind doesn't belong to you, like you got locked out of your own brain and can't find the keys.

When you lie in that hospital bed, you retrace your steps and try to figure it all out. You've got no experiences to relate this one to. There's just a slew of bad crime shows and that one time you acted out *One Flew over the Cuckoo's Nest* in drama class. Other than that, you have no other opinions except that you like the socks. The socks they've given you are nice. Will you get to keep the socks?

The doctor asks you questions and you feel like every question may be an accusation, like he is watching you closely and wanting you to say something compromising. You feel broken in that moment, unfixable.

You feel defined by all the questions and want to scream, grab the doctor's shoulders, and yell in his ear, "Wait, this isn't me! I had a life before this. I laughed before this. I did stuff—important stuff—before this."

But your darkness will just laugh at your sad attempts to seem sane and say something snarky like, "Toots, no one cares about that story anymore. You're mine."

You feel like all of society is functioning just fine and you're the person who can't seem to get it together. You feel guilty for everything you're putting your friends and family through, guilty that telling yourself to "just get stronger" isn't working. The lies are thick and strong at this point. At one point, you want to say you might hurt yourself just so you can stay there and not have to leave.

The only confirmed diagnosis he will give you that day is one you already know: severe depression. You will be referred to an inpatient program, and you and your mother will spend the next day in the waiting room of that clinic.

Doctors will lead you in and out of offices, all around the center. You will sign papers and agree to things you don't fully understand. Little by little, with no subtlety really, you will start to piece together the fact that maybe you're not going back to Atlanta. You're going to stay here and get better. You are going to say good-bye to the life you thought God was calling you toward and you will wonder, probably for a long while, if you ever really heard him.

That's what happens in the dark sometimes: You doubt the voice of God. You doubt the plans. You wonder if he's really coming for you, if anyone is really going to show up and pull you out of the mess.

In that waiting room, you're surrounded by all kinds of characters. One guy looks like a clone of Prince but with really sketchy eyes that dart back and forth like he's watching for something. An older gentleman paces the floor—back and forth, back and forth—slurring as saliva shoots out of his mouth. You cannot make out what he is saying. You just want him to sit down. Another man keeps getting up from his seat, charging into the breezeway and picking up the pay phone. He screams and cusses into the pay phone, slams it down on the receiver, and moves back inside. He sits, crosses his arms, and huffs loudly.

The man beside him looks exhausted and tired. That's the first time you cry—when you look at the men sitting side by side and wonder who they are together. A father and a son? Two friends? A counselor and a patient?

Your pride takes a hit as you sit in the waiting room, thinking to yourself, *This isn't my life. This cannot be my life. I don't deserve to be here. Other people have done far worse. I've done everything right.*

That's not the point. The point isn't to compare yourself to someone else's life in this moment. If the moral of the story was "do good, and nothing bad will ever happen to you," the book of Job would never be a thing. Life still happens. Pain still comes. Mental illness still roars.

The depression wants this to be a story about you. You, you, you. When you look back on the illness, when you see it from a ten-thousand-foot view, you will want to scream over the amount of "you" in the story. Depression is a liar. If the waiting room does nothing more that day than teach you how to say a single prayer for someone else in this battle, then it's worth it. This isn't a story that's all about you. This isn't going to be a story about you winning if you just come out of this. We *all* deserve to be free from our demons. We *all* deserve to come out of the woods.

STEAL THIS PRAYER

Dear God, why is it so hard to wait? Teach me to wait on you, to not expect some instant gratification but to see beauty in the times where things are slower and I can't really predict what will come next. Show me growth when all I see is an hourglass. Teach me to wait on your love.

| Chapter | **COUNT YOUR** |
| Eight | **VICTORIES** |

I wish I could tell you there is this one sudden moment when God swoops in like a superhero and makes all the pain go away. Like a production set wrapping up after the filming of a television season, the lights go up, the director yells "Cut! That's a wrap," and we all go home. I want to be able to tell you that you'll experience healing in an instant. It's not impossible, but there is usually more trudging through the mud than that.

A lot of times, pain builds a zip code and you live there for a while. For me, "coming out of the woods" wasn't sudden. It was a seriously gradual process. It was a whole list of things I needed to do to get better: Take medicine. Talk to people. Go to therapy. Get out of bed. Take a shower. There were elements of my faith I needed to cultivate: Sit with the Bible. Write down Scripture. Pray. Even if I didn't feel like it, I chose to do these things.

People's advice to me is tired and repetitive during this time: It's important to sit with your pain. Pain demands you learn its name. You need to shut off. Limit the distractions. Get comfortable with the waiting.

I wish I could go to the nearest McDonald's and order a full recovery off the dollar menu. But then I remember God and how he wants us all to stop running and start living, even in the imperfect circumstances. Imperfect circumstances don't mean your life stops. Sometimes imperfect circumstances cause your life to truly begin.

"Okay, new plan," my friend Chrisy says to me one morning as we meet up at her home. She is one of the women dedicated to seeing me every day through this depression until it lifts. I am making traction at this point. I am starting to feel the medication working and I am getting stronger.

"Let me ask you this: When you went through depression that first time, what brought you out of it?"

The answer has always been pretty obvious to me. I did a TED talk in 2012 that went viral, and since then, I've never been able to separate myself from the girl who left love letters across New York City to cope with depression.

"I wrote letters to strangers," I said. "You know this."

"You stopped thinking about yourself," she said.

"Yeah, and it helped."

"So go home and write more letters," she said to me. "This time, I want you to write letters to people you know. You don't have to write to strangers anymore. There are so many people who have been with you in this fight. You haven't thanked them yet."

Chrisy told me to begin writing down all of my steps and accomplishments. She said depression was going to try to trick me into thinking I wasn't making any improvements, but if I wrote down all the little things I did on a daily basis, I'd start to see the progress. She told me to call them my "little victories."

"Even when you write a letter, record the task. Every letter you write is a big step toward doing something other than admitting defeat."

This is what I needed. I didn't need someone to stroke my head and pity me for being depressed. I needed someone to tell me to get up and do something. And then do something else. And then something else.

I stopped by Target on my way home and picked up stationery. I wrote about thirty letters that day—all to people who had been in my corner for this fight. I found myself driving down the street to the convenience store on the corner and buying a pack of black composition notebooks made of faux leather. At home, I wrote on the front of one of them the words "Fight Song 2015" in thick silver Sharpie.

I decided I wanted to write fight songs—little notes of encouragement—into this black notebook for my daughter who doesn't exist yet. I can't actually say I'll ever have a daughter, but I've been writing these "nonexistent child" letters for years about falling in love, being brave, and going after what makes you come alive.

I started writing these notes when I was about thirteen years old after I discovered my mother's diaries in the back of our family's bookcase. One by one, I snuck a diary out of the bookcase and brought it to my bedroom to read about my mother and a life she lived before me. Even though she didn't write in those diaries for me, I felt like she did. I started keeping diaries religiously after that day.

I think my daughter will need something more though. On the days when she forgets how to sing, she's going to need something more robust than a diary entry. This is where the fight songs come in.

Fight songs are a reminder to keep going. Just keep going. Keep going when the storm comes. Keep going when the night falls. Keep going when the cancer arrives. Keep going when the loved ones leave. Keep going when your heart breaks. Keep going when the bottom drops out from underneath you and you don't know how to trust anymore. Keep going when you don't know what you want anymore. Keep going when the sun burns you and when people burn you (because both will happen). Keep going when you crush your dreams with the weight of your own expectations. Keep going when you don't know where to go or which place to call home anymore.

Just keep going. There's still some fight left in you.

We need the fight songs for the days when we forget how to sing. They remind us where our strength lies. They push us to be stronger.

Fight Song #4:

I just hope you always know you deserve beautiful things. You deserve the chance to close chapters and write new endings and cry loud and not be sorry for whatever makes that wild heart of yours beat.

What I hope you'll never possess—a timid heart. A life where you are afraid and fearful at every juncture. That is the hurdle I am working daily to overcome. It's not easy, but I must believe it's worth it.

I scrawled the words "Little Victories" at the top of one of the pages in the Fight Song journal.

There I began recording all my little steps. I could perform little acts. I wrote down the letters I'd written. I wrote down the emails I'd responded to. I wrote down how a friend reached out and asked if I could help her write a paper that was due the next day.

We met up at a diner and ate eggs and toast, and I helped her outline her paper and flesh out the bigger concepts. The diner date had nothing to do with me. In fact, I don't think I even brought up the depression. Instead, I helped. I exited myself and helped someone else.

I came into the house that evening feeling better than I had in months. There was something to these little victories. There was definitely something to these small steps on repeat. They became small steps out of the dark toward something bright. I needed that reminder constantly—keep counting your small victories. I have to believe if you stay faithful in counting the little wins, eventually the bigger victory will come.

Reading and writing seem to help, so I do more of them. One afternoon, in the midst of counting my victories, I buy a book on prayer by Tim Keller.[1] Despite having only one eye to work with, I start reading. I don't even realize that I am coming to a turning point as I begin to fill my brain with something other than doubt, worry, and anxiety. Every time I open that book on prayer, I am shoving those raw emotions out of the way and making space for something more than fear. I start reading all the time.

My mentor Carol tells me this is how I will start thinking different thoughts. I need to read things that are better than what's in any television show, any Netflix marathon, or any glossy magazine. She tells me I need to start feeding my brain with better things.

At a Starbucks in Connecticut, she sits with me and opens

---

1. Tim Keller, *Prayer: Experiencing Awe and Intimacy with God* (New York: Dutton, 2014).

her Bible to the book of Psalms. The first psalm is about being a tree planted by the water. She tells me to write the psalm down and to keep writing things down. I don't realize it at the time, but this is the active process of renewing your mind. Renewing your mind isn't a onetime thing. It's a rinse and repeat process. It's long hours poring over the psalms until they seep into your spirit and change your thinking patterns.

"You know you have to go back to Georgia," she tells me. This is her second time telling me that I have to go back. At this point, I find myself getting comfortable with Connecticut. I am getting stronger, but I am avoiding going back to Atlanta.

"You have to stop letting people coddle you and take care of you or you're never going to leave."

I agree with her reluctantly. People are keeping me on a schedule, making sure I am surrounded throughout a given day. I love them for this, for not leaving me behind. But I'm not living my life anymore; I'm watching other people participate in theirs and showing up as a silent observer.

"This isn't how the story ends," Carol tells me. "Maybe you go back to Atlanta and tie up the loose ends, and then you decide you want to come back to Connecticut. That's okay. But it's not time for that yet. You need to go back there and finish the story."

I know she is right. I want to pick a different ending than the one I already know by heart. I want to be someone who stops running. To be that kind of person, I think you need to change the narrative at some point.

The realization hits me on Valentine's Day in the middle of the Charlotte airport coming back from a speaking engagement at a community college in Illinois. There's an hour left in my layover. I'm blind in one eye in Charlotte on Valentine's Day. It cannot get more depressing than this. The plan is to fly back to Atlanta and people will meet me there. We will get a U-Haul, pack up my life, and say good-bye to Georgia. I can't look at my life for too long without feeling like it had been hijacked by a stranger.

As I wheel my suitcase through the terminal, I am getting phone calls every couple of minutes from concerned friends, my mom, and other people who want to make sure I am okay and getting on the plane. Doing anything at this point was an all-swim experience. I never missed a speaking engagement or event during this depression because other people helped me honor the commitments. It would have never been possible without people coaching me through airports and car rides and talking to me while I was alone in hotel rooms at night.

I plant my bag at the departing gate for Atlanta. I breathe deep and mumble the words beneath my breath, "I just want to go back to normal."

These are words I've said before. I said them first at the beginning of the depression. I called up my friend Clifton and cried out to him, "I just want to go back to normal. Why can't I just go back to normal?"

"I hate to tell you this, but your normal is what got you into this place," he said to me calmly. "When a tree gets struck by lightning, it never goes back to normal. You're going to have to build a new kind of normal."

When I huff those words "I just want to go back to normal" in the airport, I get the answer nearly immediately to my complaint: *But you weren't happy then. You've never really been happy with the "normal" you had. You've experienced bits and pieces of joy, but it hasn't been long-lasting. It's left you wanting more. It's left you here—being a spectator in your life but not a participant.*

Now is the moment to decide: Am I going to fight to build a new normal, or am I giving up? Am I going to go back to Atlanta and finish the story, like Carol told me to, or am I going to hand the pen to fear and let it keep drawing the map for me?

I call my mom before boarding the plane and tell her I'm not coming home. I say it calmly. I tell her I cannot let the story end this way. I must finish the story in Atlanta. There's a chance it will end the same. There's a chance it won't work. But I won't know if I just give up, pack my things, and leave without trying.

It is time to grow up and grow my roots down.

STEAL THIS PRAYER

Dear God, sometimes I want to quit and give up. I want to believe in you though. I want to believe my life is not an accident and my struggles are seen and understood. Help me to stay in the fight. Grow endurance in me. Make me stronger, braver, and wiser as I go. Show me others who are in the fight too. Help me take that next step and let go of the rest.

| Chapter Nine | # DO WHAT DOT DID |

In 2015, David Brooks published a piece in the *New York Times* called "The Moral Bucket List."[1] He realized throughout the last few years that he kept coming across people who had some sort of internal light.

Brooks wrote about Dorothy Day in the piece. Before I read that article, I didn't know who Dorothy Day was, but she was a prominent religious activist. There's even talk of her becoming a saint one day.

Dorothy Day used to be someone completely different though. Earlier in her life, she was a drinker and very disorganized. She struggled to see the meaning in life, attempting suicide twice. And then Day became pregnant with her daughter, and everything changed. She became decentered in the sense that it wasn't about her anymore. The love she felt spreading across her body at the birth of her daughter made it impossible to deny the existence of God. That love propelled her to root her life. Brooks writes of Day, "She made unshakable commitments in all directions." She joined a church. She started writing for a newspaper. She worked out her faith. She raised her daughter.

---

1. David Brooks, "The Moral Bucket List," *New York Times*, April 11, 2015, www.nytimes.com/2015/04/12/opinion/sunday/david-brooks-the-moral-bucket -list.html.

I think about Dorothy Day a lot. My mom and I like to imagine that we are close friends with her. We call her "Dot" for short. If Dot and I were really hanging out all the time, I would ask her where she started first, like, if she began with making her bed, or did she try to add more spinach into her diet.

I'm fascinated by people like Dot, who change their own lives through acts of discipline. You think it's some unexplainable magic until you start trying to become disciplined yourself and realize it's simpler than you think. That's what I'd tell people if they asked me how I started to build a new life after depression. I did what Dot did: I made unshakable commitments in all directions.

———

The unshakable commitments began with eggs. Start really small, right? It starts with calling my friend Jenna one night and telling her I want to go to Waffle House and eat eggs. Jenna is someone who is never fazed by my requests, never going to think I'm crazy for wanting to try something new.

You may think eggs are ridiculous, but I believe they're the perfect starting place for someone who is trying to build a life they want. The key word is *want*. When I dated Caleb a year earlier, I had such a hard time figuring out what I wanted. I remember one time when he told me he was going to build me a desk. I was tickled by the thought of some guy building me a desk—until he asked me what I wanted the desk to look like. How many drawers did I want? What structure did I prefer? You'd think I was making momentous decisions, given how I was flipping out over the questions. My mom reminded me several times, "It's just a desk. It's just a desk." Yet I never did figure out what I wanted my desk to look like. I only ever dreamed about the desk but never got clear on what I wanted.

"Why are we going to eat eggs?" Jenna asks.

"Because it matters," I tell her. "It matters to know how you like your eggs."

When we are sitting at one of the Waffle House tables with laminated menus in front of us, I tell Jenna why eggs are so important. I tell her there's a movie called *Runaway Bride*.

In the movie, Julia Robert's character is completely indecisive. She figures out what she wants out of life based on who she dates and who she eventually gets engaged to. Every wedding ends up being the same thing: guy stands at the altar waiting, Julia never shows up. She literally runs away from every wedding scene. She becomes known as the girl who runs away from every little thing that scares her.

Spoiler alert: Turns out that she's not afraid of the lives other people could build for her; she's afraid to build a life all on her own. She's afraid of doing the hard work of building an identity outside of a person who defines her. So after bolting out of her last wedding, Julia goes back to the basics and decides she is going to figure out how she likes her eggs. Poached. Runny. Over easy. Over medium. She's going to figure it out.

At some point, you decide to get over your fear. You say it's time to not be afraid of whatever decisions you have to make or direction you need to take. So for Jenna and me, that first decision begins with eggs.

"I'm ordering every egg," I tell the guy taking our order. "Every egg you've got on the menu, I want to try it."

The guy is totally into this. He's listing egg choices and insisting that egg with cheese on top is also a choice. The eggs come out from the kitchen with four on one plate and four on the other. The poached egg sits in the center of one of the plates. I pick up a fork and start working, biting into egg after egg.

Some of the eggs are runny. Some are hard when I dig a fork into them. They do not budge. A few of the eggs are a scrambled selection. After a while, all eggs start to taste the same, so it really just comes down to the consistency and the presentation of the eggs you like. After fifteen minutes of eating eggs, Jenna taking small bites alongside me, I make my decision: I like my eggs sunny-side up and "dipping eggs," as they call it. I like to dip my toast into my eggs.

Eggs don't solve the world's problems, this I know. But I think there is something powerful about knowing what you want and becoming really sure of it. Eggs are the small choice, but maybe you graduate to toast later. Then you move on to picking a pair of shoes you like. Then you become sure of the kind of music you want to listen to. Then you make better decisions when dating and meeting a match. The whole point is making a choice because it's the thing you love, not what someone else told you to love.

The second thing that happens, after the eggs, is honesty. Honesty is harder to master than poached eggs. I first try my hand at honesty one Monday night after the bachelor has given out all his roses for the evening.

When I first moved to Atlanta, my friend Eryn and I would get together with a girl named Anna on Monday evenings and watch *The Bachelor*. They were my first real friends, and even though I didn't watch the show to begin with, I liked having people to make plans with. We painted our nails, ate cheese, clinked little glasses of champagne, and watched someone try to find love on national television. The more we showed up, the bigger the group became.

We are all in our mid-twenties to early thirties. We are all working and trying to juggle personal life. Some have families. Some are pregnant. We get together every Monday night to watch girls and guys pass out roses. We laugh. We crack jokes. These are sacred times—not because of the one on the screen who's looking for love, but because of the community we build after every episode, through every group text, and between every commercial break.

It wasn't always this way though. I don't want to give the wrong idea that community with other people is instant or easy. There were multiple times, and there still are, when I'd rather sit at home on my couch alone than bake an appetizer and hang out with people after a long day. It's hard to stay committed to people. Consistency isn't an easy thing. Yet I'm learning when you stay and don't give up the moment you find yourself wanting to, the breakthrough usually comes. You bust through some fourth wall you didn't know was there and forge something real with other people.

Back to the honesty. It is just a few weeks after I decide to stay in Atlanta and fight to build my new normal. The episode of *The Bachelor* has just ended. A few people have left.

I seize the moment to be honest. "Half the time, I don't want to be here," I admit to the group. "And I also don't feel like I know who I really am."

I tell them I found a way to live on the surface for the last eight months or so, being careful not to let anyone in. People don't want your stiff, two-dimensional images of yourself though. They want something real.

The girls in the room aren't shocked or fazed. They know, and it's as if they have been waiting for me to be the honest one. When I tell them I want to figure out who I am, no one thinks I'm crazy. In fact, a few of the girls who are a few years older have walked through the very same thing. It's an identity shift. It's figuring out who you are and what you want and where you need to be to make those things permanent. It's figuring out who are the people who will stand on the sideline and cheer for you. These are mine. You think you're all alone until suddenly you're not anymore.

From that night come coffee dates I want to cancel and gestures to serve my friends in ways I don't really want to. I realize love—building it and making it last—is doing a lot of the things you don't really feel like doing. A lot of times, something in your heart eventually changes and you get into a good rhythm. You start to love the feeling of showing up for people when they need you. I offer my babysitting services to two friends. I offer writing services to another friend. I start sitting in on a small group at my church with eight other girls who are younger than me. We meet at coffee shops around Atlanta and dig through the Bible, and I feel a sense of ownership. They want to know about dating guys and how to get up earlier. This is the stuff that matters to them. I answer questions. I lead them to places in the Bible where I know God answers.

It turns out that people need us in the simplest and most mundane ways, but we miss it if we don't stay long enough. We miss out on serving someone. I learn as the weeks go by that something happens when you say yes and you let a new person in. "Yes" is a powerful statement. "Okay, I won't run" is a powerful statement. "Come in and see my baggage"—that's powerful too.

I would tell you to say yes to things that scare you, even if you aren't sure where they'll lead. My friend Mary once told me, "If it's not a 'heck yes,' then it's a 'heck no.'" She was referring to love and dating. It was her rule of thumb.

I treated that advice like it was on the inside cover of the Bible. I went out into the world looking for every "heck yes." The certainty. The brave and bold and undeniable assurance. I believed in the "heck yes" for a really long time, and I don't as much anymore.

There's just one issue to the "heck yes" litmus test: Not every "heck yes" is born overnight. You meet people and you want to write them off, but you find out, a few weeks or a few months in, that they're really very good for you. You start a job and you think it's your dream job, but then you wake up a few years later and realize your "heck yes" has dried up.

It takes a while for a "heck yes" to grow and become reliable. It takes time and grace. You have to plant your "heck yes" in the ground, and then you also need to be okay with it maybe not working out. I think you choose your "heck yes," just like you choose your life. You choose it hourly. Daily. It gets stronger as you go. Your choices hold more weight when you continue doing just that—choosing them again and again.

I am still in process. Hopefully, that will always be the case. So I remind myself pretty much daily: Don't shut the door just yet. Don't cut out too early. You're just at the beginning. Keep choosing. Take the expectations and the pressure off yourself. Rewrite the story with less fear in this draft. Maybe it's not about knowing what you want. Maybe it's about making slow and steady choices to become a better character in the story.

As you keep showing up, your commitments will become

unshakable. You'll be like Dot. Your commitments will likely turn you into a more honest person. And then, almost like it formed out of nowhere, you become a consistent person, and consistent people are very hard to find in the world today.

As I pressed in harder to commitments, I devoted myself to the college group at the church I'd been going to every Sunday in Atlanta. The college group is a place for people between the ages of eighteen and twenty-five to hang out and talk about God. I say I "devoted myself" because I technically joined the group when I moved to Atlanta nearly a year earlier to feel more a part of something, but I'd never really dug in. I stayed on the fringes. I didn't invest. I was flaky.

I love my generation, but we are flaky sometimes. I've had several conversations with people my age who say the reason it's so tough to build relationships or keep them going is because we come into them with only half of our hearts sometimes. We like to keep one foot out the door in case a better option comes along.

I used to be guilty of this. I would make plans with someone, but I would be flaky about the confirmation. We'd leave the time or the place open-ended. There were plenty of times when, as the meet-up approached, I'd pray that they would duck out. I'm learning you miss out on a lot of things in life when you are indecisive about your yes. Saying yes and following through builds a lot of character. It makes you a reliable person.

I had to place the habit of flakiness—as sacred as it felt to me—on the altar and sacrifice it to the gods of consistency once I decided to stay in Atlanta. Sometimes you don't even realize how much people need you to show up.

My circles became smaller, and I ended up fostering community in this college group with a few different girls from around the city.

One of these girls is Brooke. Brooke is new to Atlanta, like me, and going to grad school here. She is at the cusp of the transition, and so I know to tell her that the first year is definitely the hardest. I tell her not to be disheartened by this but to keep going. Something really beautiful happens when you begin staying with things.

Brooke is Texas Proud. She talks about it constantly, and I love that about her. She also runs a lot. She has a goal of running ten races in ten different countries. So far, she's run one in Haiti, and when I met her, she was training for a marathon in Nashville. I watched her begin and follow through with the training. She had a goal and was sticking with it. She wasn't giving up.

As she approached her first twenty-mile run, I asked Brooke if she wanted me to get out of bed and run alongside her for that first mile. I'm not a big runner, so I can't promise much more than that. She beamed when I brought it up, and we arranged to meet at the starting line.

"Hey," I texted her the night before, "do you want me to meet you at the finish line instead? To run the last mile with you?"

It hit me as I squashed my own pre-running nerves that I have no problem *starting* anything. It's the *finishing* part that leaves me feeling defeated and alone. I think this world is good at preaching beginnings to us, but it neglects showing us how to finish strong. I want to be someone who finishes strong. I want to be the kind of person who shows up for people at the end of the story, not just at the beginning.

Brooke says we need to go all-in to whatever event, meeting, or task is at hand. Even if you're headed for a messy situation, go all-in to the mess. So that's what I do. I go all in. And it's messy. Brooke and I were set to meet at mile nineteen the next morning. When I found her at the agreed-upon location, she wasn't at mile nineteen. She was actually on mile fifteen, a few miles behind her scheduled destination, but she hadn't given up. I began running alongside her and cheering her on.

At this point, Brooke was mentally done. She wanted to give up and go home to a hot shower and her bed.

"Giving up is not an option," I screamed in my loudest pep-talk voice. "You do not get to give up. You get to meet this goal."

We made it to mile sixteen and then seventeen. At mile eighteen, Brooke asked if we could give up. Could we call it a victory at mile eighteen?

Here's the thing: You can absolutely call mile eighteen a victory. Heck, mile two is a victory for me. But I know the personality of Brooke. Brooke is the kind of individual who wants to meet her goals, even if you have to drag her to the finish line. She isn't a quitter, and so in that moment, quitting couldn't be an option for me to give her. I had to remind her she was capable when everything in her brain told her she was not.

I think we forget that people look to us for answers like that. They want to know they can keep going. They want to know you're not quitting on them. That doesn't mean we become God to them or the only voice of wisdom, but we have a unique opportunity to speak truth into the lives of people who love us. We get to help people to the finish line. We get to stand in the face of some pretty loud lies and tell someone, "I won't let you give up. I'm not going anywhere."

Somehow—though I don't know how—I ended up running the last five miles with Brooke. She collapsed into the grass the second her watch flashed "20 miles." I stayed with her. Cheered with her. Fought through the pain with her. There were really surreal instances throughout the run when I realized I could not shoulder her pain; I could only stand with her. That's a really strange feeling—to see a person hurting beside you and not be able to do anything but stay. In these moments, I wish a manual would drop down from heaven called "How to Stay . . . Even When You Think Your Presence Doesn't Help Anything." That would be a super useful manual. It should probably be required reading for those of us who want to be better humans.

But I promise you it is worth it to run toward victory with someone else. It is worth it to meet mountains together and battle to the finish line. That's what life is—a battle. It's gritty. It's sometimes merciless. But it is painfully beautiful in the moments when we take our eyes off ourselves and focus them on our purpose. I think our purpose is to just show up to the moment we've been invited into, the moments other people ask us to come and inhabit with them. We get to be mile markers and cheerleaders. We get to hold signs. We get to have so much purpose when we just look around.

This life is tough and it throws frequent punches, but I don't want to miss my chance to show up at mile nineteen. If I don't show up, I'll never know if someone needed me to help them cross the finish line.

STEAL THIS PRAYER

Dear God, I know you are in the dotted lines, not just the destinations. Uproot this thing in me that needs clarity and directions all the time and just show me how to make unshakable commitments in all directions. I want to be a consistent person. Give me good work to do and good people to cross the finish line with.

Chapter Ten	# BE HERE NOW

A reader emailed me once to tell me about her recent experience of being ghosted. Not having ever heard this term, I read on. She wrote to tell me how she had been seeing this guy for a few weeks. They were going on dates and things seemed to be looking good. And then—out of nowhere—he ghosted her.

Ghosting in this context means he stopped texting her back. He blocked her from social media accounts. He went on with his life as if she had never been a part of it. Ghosting is a method of getting rid of someone—exiting the relationship—without going through any of the hard feelings or awkward conversations that come from cutting things off the right way. You simply become a ghost and disappear from someone's life. You delete them.

When I finished reading the email, I called a few friends who are a little younger than I am to confirm or deny whether ghosting really happens. They tell me it is far more common than we would want to believe.

For a long time, I thought God was ghosting me. I only heard from him in spurts, and I figured maybe he just wasn't there anymore. My oldest friend Corey and I don't talk every day. We can go weeks without saying a word to one another, but then, when either of us calls, we pick up where we left off. When it comes to God, I assume it must be over if there's been some distance. I assume everything we've built crumbled when I wasn't looking. I know I'm not the only person who has ever felt like God packed a suitcase in the middle of the night and hustled out of the picture.

When I was going through depression, my mother and I both wondered quite often where God was. My mom went on prayer walks around the neighborhood and told me that one time she felt that God spoke clearly to her and just said, "I've got this."

My mother was so confused about that. She searched the Scriptures to no avail. The words "I've got this" don't appear once. She wanted to hear from God. She wanted to know if this was just her mind dishing up some slang, or if God really did have it. No matter how hard she prayed though, that was the phrase that kept repeating itself to her: "I've got this. I've got this."

But why wasn't he releasing me from the pain? Why wasn't he making me better? We ask these questions when something bad happens to someone we love. We don't understand—we can't seem to wrap our little brains around—a God who lets bad things happen. There's so much in the world to make us wonder where God is: death, heartbreak, the nightly news. It's not really a stretch to imagine ourselves living in a world where God unfriended us on Facebook and proceeded to wipe away any trace of a relationship he ever had with us.

That's what I remember as the harshest emotion at the beginning of the depression—the jagged fear that God was going to stay silent, that God was punishing me for a bunch of past stuff I'd done and this was his holy revenge. When everything came crashing down on November 18, I had to figure out whether God caused the depression. Whether it was punishment, or something that God would use as a part of my story. I had to trust in a benevolent God, or I probably wasn't going to make it out of the woods.

For a lot of people, that's why they refuse to believe in God in the first place. With any person I've ever talked to about God, in cases where they didn't believe in him, it's always the question that gets asked in the first ten minutes: So where is God in the suffering? Why does he let bad things happen?

I don't know. I honestly don't have a solid answer for the exact coordinates of God's presence in times of suffering, but I think he shows up most fully in people. He makes himself known in people who don't realize they're beacons of light in their own imperfect ways, helping other people find their way home.

I don't understand why God allows the suffering, but I know he sends people into the dark to do the holding and the talking and the tea making on his behalf. And once you suffer through the darkness and come out on the other side, you learn that one day the most important role you'll ever get to play is when it's your turn to hold someone, listen to them, and make them tea. It will be one of the most unseen roles you've ever assumed, and there will be no way to glorify it or call attention to it with a selfie. The role will be quiet and messy. The role will be weird and a little disjointed. You'll see sides of your family and friends you never hoped to see. You will know weakness in a new way.

I want to say that in the midst of suffering, God isn't ghosting us. He isn't scanning Kayak.com for one-way trips away from us. He isn't failing to see us or hear us. He isn't ghosting us; he might just be showing up differently than we expected.

———

My friend Erika believes there is no place too lowly or inauspicious for God to show up. He's present. He's everywhere. He's at McDonald's. He's at the gym. He's at the bus stop. He's right here.

As I make my decision to stay in Atlanta, I realize I need to trust this more. I now believe God will be with me in the dark, but I wonder how he will show up when things get mundane again. Where is God when life stops impressing us and we actually do learn how to walk in everyday life?

I have two buddies in Atlanta who own a space that doubles as a coffee shop and a place for people who love motorcycles. They say anyone is invited, and they really mean it. I started spending more time at the motorcycle space when I decided to stay in Atlanta because it pushes me out of my isolation. I bring mail to the post office for them. I help them with small errands. I hang out some evenings when I don't feel like going home. And one night, I'm standing in a circle with a bunch of guys when one motions for me to come over to his bike.

"Come on," he says to me. "We're going for a ride."

"This isn't really my thing," I tell him. I'm scared of everything, really.

He isn't listening though. He waits for me to get a helmet and tells me to get on the back of the bike.

Soon after, we are riding. I am holding on to him tightly and I am screaming. It occurs to me in the moment just how much fear I have inside me. Every word is fearful, and I need to let some stuff go. I need to trust more.

"Okay," he yells over the motor, "we're going to take a turn up ahead."

I'm thinking to myself, *Why does this matter? Why is he telling me this?*

"When we turn left, I need you to lean left with me, okay?"

I am terrified at his request. I think the bike will flip. I don't have another option though. He isn't slowing down and we are going to turn left.

"Okay?" he yells.

I nod from the back of the bike and confirm it.

I am worried he will mess it up. I am worried we will go down and get battered. I am worried that we won't make the turn. He will let me down. I will have had all the right reasons to be so afraid. Regardless of if I'm ready, we turn left.

He leans. I lean.

We make it.

Again we turn left.

He leans. I lean.

My grip around him loosens. We are in a straightaway and I raise up one hand in the air to let the wind trickle through my fingers. I laugh for the first time in a really long time. We go over a speed bump and I don't flinch. After the third or fourth bump, I stop noticing the rise we get in the air.

I realize in that moment, with the night air so intoxicating and the engine roaring loudly, that if I ever want to enjoy this journey, I'm going to need to learn how to trust. How to let go. How to admit I'm not in control. I am not the driver; I am just the one who leans left. I need to trust. I need to live like there's a left turn coming up and I'm expected to lean into it. I need to trust that God will be here to cover the rest.

_____

So how? How do I expand the trust and learn to see God more in the here and now? I honestly think a lot of it comes down to prayer.

As I walked out of that depression, I became really serious about prayer. Like, really obsessed. Prayer is like a lung—we need it. No compromise. No cutting corners. And yet Prayer 101 doesn't exist. I search through the Bible for references to prayer and see that James was a pray-er, a trait that earned him the nickname "the man with camel's knees."[1] People called him Old Camel's Knees because he spent so much time praying—so much time that his knees hardened like those of a camel. It's not the most flattering nickname, but it's certainly bold. I mean, imagine someone calling you out in a crowd and saying, "That one prays so much." "That one is a warrior." "That one isn't afraid to say she needs God more than anything." If I were as cool as James, I would flaunt my camel's knees.

I am nothing like James, but I want to be. I don't want to pray for things like they're an ultimatum, constantly testing God in the hope that he'll be kind to me. I know God is kind. I know he moves. I want to pray prayers that push me aside. So in an effort to stretch my faith, I pray one morning, "God, send me someone who needs me today."

At the end of my time with the Bible, I write a reminder on my hand so I won't walk away from my journal and forget my bold prayer. I write the words "someone is coming" on my palm. This is definitely the stupidest thing to write on the palm of your hand. I immediately have a morbid vision of me in some back alleyway, conked out, and someone running up to me, only to notice the words "someone is coming" scrawled on the palm of my hand. That's the start of a Lifetime movie.

I go to my office space. I pick up groceries. I go to Target,

---

1. Herbert Lockyer, *All the Men of the Bible* (Grand Rapids: Zondervan, 1958), 170–71.

because Target always feels like a good idea, and in the middle of the stationery aisle, I look down at my palm and notice I've written something on my hand. I have no idea what it is. That is how easily I forget my prayers.

I remind myself, once I make out the faded handwriting, that someone is coming. Someone is going to need me. I check my inbox again. No email that implies I'm needed in the way I want to be needed. "I want to save the day, God. Don't you see that? Use me to save the day!"

As I continue walking through the aisles of Target, my phone starts buzzing in my pocket. It's my neighbor Dimitri. I debated letting it go to voice mail. If it's actually important, he'll leave a voice mail. A few seconds later: *you have one new voice mail.*

I listen and call him back a few seconds in. He and his wife need a last-minute babysitter for the following evening. It's a huge favor, since their babysitter backed out. I tell him I'm free and available to babysit. Of course I will babysit.

I look down at my hand again as I'm talking to him and read the words "someone is coming." This is not what I meant when I said my prayer earlier this morning for someone to need me.

And yet throughout the rest of that day, Dimitri is the only person who actually needs me. No crazy traumatic email ever arrives into my inbox. No insane "you won't believe what happened to me" story occurs that will allow me to dramatically retell the story to my friends later on. Just Dimitri, my neighbor who I see nearly every morning at my favorite coffee shop, asking if I'd be willing to babysit Penny the following night.

I want to wrestle God on this one and tell him we had some parameters for this prayer of mine. I want to tell him about my expectations and the hopes I had inside me when I wrote down that prayer. But I know what God would probably say: *An answered prayer is an answered prayer. You should just be thankful that you're needed by someone today.* God knows where he needs me to fill in the gaps, and if I don't think the job is good enough, then he can just go find someone else.

I'm learning that a lot of life happens in the unseen stuff. So much of the places where our lives will actually matter have to do with acts unseen by the world. They are the things we never document. I think that happens on purpose. I don't think God needs us to pat ourselves on the back and commend ourselves for being such solid human beings. I think he'd probably rather say, *Listen, I need you to pay attention. Eyes up. If you're always wondering how you can document your life just perfectly, you won't succeed at truly living it.*

So what if the constant prayer is "be here now"? What if that was the prayer to invite God in? Every good story begins with an invitation. What more might we see in this hurting world if we told God we wanted him here?

When you pray the "be here now" prayer, crazy things start to happen. I need to give you a little bit of a backstory for you to see just how crazy it is. When I was in high school, I was obsessed with *The Devil Wears Prada.* I read the book several times and then graduated to the movie. I am a little embarrassed to admit that when I moved to New York after college, I prayed frequently, "God, give me a scene from *The Devil Wears Prada.*" That's not a normal prayer. I honestly don't know what an answer to that sort of prayer would have looked like. I think

I just wanted to feel like a real New Yorker, making it out there in the big world, standing gutsy and tall in high heels against the odds during a year that felt transitional and uneasy. While living in New York, I never got that moment.

After I began to plant my roots in Atlanta and make it my own, I was brought back to New York City for the launch of my first book. I was getting better by the day, but I was still pretty fragile. I felt like I was taking these steps forward, but at the end of the day, there was still an unrelenting desire to look back and wonder if it would happen all over again. Would the darkness pull me back in? Am I safe?

I flew back to Connecticut. I saw my family and friends. I got to have this really sweet moment where I gathered so many of the people who fought through the depression with me, and over tacos and queso we celebrated what God had done. There's no better way to celebrate. I looked around the table at one point and felt nothing but gratitude. No fear, just thankfulness. We'd fought a crazy battle together, and somehow we won.

I took a train into New York the next day—the day of my book release. A town car picked me up from my hotel that evening to drive me to my first book signing in SoHo. We drove the thirty minutes to the bookstore, and I didn't say a word to the driver. He tried to start several conversations but eventually gave up on me. I sat in the back of the car, feeling anxious and nauseous, reluctant to have any sort of conversation. I was nervous and stuck inside my own head.

"I'll be right here when you get done," the driver told me when we arrived at the back entrance of the bookstore. I nodded and thanked him as I headed toward the door. I didn't ask for his name.

Following the signing, the driver took me to the restaurant where we were celebrating the release. He was waiting for me again when dinner was over and it was time to go back to the hotel.

My parents asked if they could ride in the town car with me. My father asked the man if he minded making a detour to take them to Grand Central Station to catch their train home.

He agreed and welcomed them in. My mother and he started chatting on the ride to the train station as if they were best friends. Turns out that the driver's name was Eric. He was Italian. Very Italian. He lived on Long Island. He was an actor. This thrilled my mother.

"Anything we might have seen?" I asked.

"I've been in a few things, like *Law & Order* and *The Sopranos*," he said. "I don't know if you've ever seen *The Devil Wears Prada*?"

My mouth dropped open.

"I was the driver for Anne Hathaway's character."

"You were the town car driver in *The Devil Wears Prada*?" I asked in disbelief.

"Yes, that was me," he said. "I played Roy. I drove around Anne Hathaway, and the coolest part was they didn't even have to train me for the job because I was already a driver."

The Internet Movie Database tells me Eric played several drivers in several different series, like *The Sopranos* and *Law & Order*, but his most notable role was Roy in *The Devil Wears Prada*.

And here I was, squished in the back of a town car next to my parents, getting the closest thing possible. I mean, what are the odds that out of all the drivers in New York City, I'd be in the backseat being driven around by the one driver who drove Anne Hathaway and Meryl Streep places too?

It was right there. An answered prayer. Right in front of me. God was showing up as subtly as a driver I really didn't care about getting to know because I was too nervous and stuck in my own head. For the rest of that car ride, I thought about how I would have never come to know about Roy—never had that *The Devil Wears Prada* moment—if my mom hadn't reached out to get to know him. It makes me wonder how many other moments I'm missing out on, letting them slip past me because I'm more consumed with whatever I'm feeling. That's a battle anxiety will always make me fight for—the present moment and what God may be doing with it.

Eric dropped me off in front of my hotel. I waved good-bye. I felt lighter standing on the street that evening. I want to believe God can heal people of things like depression in an instant, but I see more that the healing takes place in increments. In little thing by little thing. I think it's how he builds our faith and makes us pay attention. He uses all the creative elements available to him, even drivers like Eric, to reach for our attention and say, "Hey, I'm right here. I haven't forgotten about you. You need to look up more though. I'm doing things. And when you're ready, I'll be right here."

STEAL THIS PRAYER

Dear God, I don't want to miss a thing. Wake me up to the world around me and show me how to live in your constant presence. I want eyes to see you in the small details, the big events, and the darkest hours. Save me from distractions so I don't miss the good parts of this lifetime.

EVACUATE THE CAMP

Chapter Eleven

Shortly after I came back to Atlanta for good, I moved out of the first home I'd lived in, since my roommate was getting married. I wanted them to have that home because it's the perfect first home. I moved into another house with a friend I made through *Bachelor* night.

In the spirit of being a home renter, and this time really embracing it, I decided to plant a garden in our backyard. In actuality, I met a guy at church one Sunday who said he gardened in all these exotic countries, and I asked him if he'd come over and help me plant a garden. Everyone thought we should date because we had a garden together. It became quite comical. We sent texts back and forth about the "kids"—which were really tomatoes and basil and a few other veggie children. I created an Instagram account for the garden called "Hannah Plus Ten," since there were ten veggie children. It was a *Jon & Kate Plus 8* kind of scenario, but my veggie daddy didn't visit his kids enough to really stay in the picture.

Sidenote: there are only two pictures on that account. I was more excited to keep the account rolling than I was to do the actual work of gardening. I learned pretty quickly that gardening isn't a joke. It's not as simple as a potted plant on the windowsill.

A ton of things go into whether a garden fails or succeeds. You learn a lot about God and how he works when you garden. You learn just how little control you really have.

Approximately two weeks after beginning my garden, I admitted defeat and put down my watering can. A few nights later, I was at a birthday party for my neighbor Rachel. Rachel is married to Dimitri. They are the couple I babysit for.

Dimitri is the most eccentric Greek guy you'll ever meet. I call him my wise, old Greek friend, and I'm sure it paints a picture in people's heads of a bald guy with a mustache and a kind smile. Dimitri is only twenty-seven and he's got a full head of hair. He gardens too.

At one point in the night, he leads me to the front yard to show me his garden and what he's got growing.

"How is yours going?" he asks.

"Not so well," I say, shrugging it off.

"I figured as much. You haven't posted anything since those first two pictures."

"I don't know how to take care of it," I admit. "I was seeing little sprouts and I was getting really excited, and then all of a sudden all these pretty little plants started growing and I couldn't keep up."

"Plants or weeds?" he asks.

"There's really a difference?"

"You have to weed the garden, Hannah."

"But they look like they'll be flowers," I say. "I figured I just needed to give it time. But now the damage is done. Your garden looks so clean, and mine is a jungle."

"They are weeds," he says. "And weeds look a lot like plants.

If you don't pull out the weeds, they will literally steal nutrients from your plants. Your plants won't get a shot at life because the weeds are taking it from them."

I thought about my little jungle of weeds in that moment, how they were maniacally strangling the life out of my little garden children while I was just an onlooker. I was basically committing murder, killing my children without even knowing it.

"You think they're harmless," he continues. "Until you realize your plants could actually grow and be much healthier if you just took the time to uproot the weeds."

"This is why I'm a writer and not a gardener," I say to him.

"Yeah," he responds, "I know you're not going to hear another word I say after this. You're going to be crafting a story in your head about me. And that's okay."

Dimitri is right. I barely listen to a thing he says about the garden from that point on as he waters the plants and checks on each one. I'm too busy thinking about the weeds and all the life they are sucking away while I just call them pretty.

I looked at my own life and realized I had a lot of weeds to uproot. I thought they were harmless, but they were keeping me from the present moment. They were telling me it was okay to disengage from this new life I was building and retreat back to my habits of isolation and fear.

Once I started looking at the excuses I was making to not let people get close, I realized what I was up against: a good deal of lies. A small army of lies that had pitched tents in my brain, built fires, and decided to camp out for a very long time.

I have to be all the things. I used to believe the lie that I could be everything to everyone. Now I know the truth: life possesses more meaning when I invest in a few.

"You can't be all the things," she says. "We all want to be all the things, and we just cannot be." This was my friend Carrie talking. I don't know how many times I wrestled in conversation over the phone with Carrie, since we live six hours away. I know I seriously don't like it at first when someone gives me the truth. I want to be invincible. I want to be able to do it all.

So this lie that "you can be all the things to all the people" was the one that started choking me first, and I had to let it go if I wanted real roots. It drove the overachiever inside me to want to show up for everyone, to do anything I possibly could. Make changes. Have a million coffee dates.

I think the danger in this is that you can be doing all the things but for the wrong reasons. You can become so obsessed with proving you can show up and be involved in everything that you start doing it to be recognized and approved of instead of doing it because your heart tells you it's right.

Putting up my hand and saying, "Don't worry, I've got this. I've got it handled," is a way for me to act like I don't need people. In my depression, that act fell hard. Most days, I couldn't even plot out a schedule of my day. I needed people. I needed people to do the holding, the cooking, the talking.

Defeating this lie looked like deliberate action steps. A lot of them. I would defeat this lie by still showing up for people (just not all the people). I would develop a close circle and begin investing slow and steady. I would stay put long enough to let people see my fears and doubts, the way my face gets beet red when I'm embarrassed, my disappointments and my scars. Action steps are my favorite thing because we live in a world where people try to make their words count for works. There's a difference though. Either you talked about being there for someone, or you actually showed up for it. Even when the lies in your brain are deafening, you can make them weaker by stepping out into action.

I started asking girlfriends out to coffee, and before the coffee date was over, I'd plan another time to meet up. This kept me focusing on a few friendships rather than trying to maintain them all. People become constant in your life that way. You build trust, and then you really end up living life together.

I cooked meals for my neighbors and signed up for meal trains when babies were born. I learned how to use a slow cooker and started showing up at my friends' doors with leftovers. I opened up in conversations with people who felt safe because I realized you cannot build trust without entrusting something to someone else. This is the hardest one for me because there's the fear in the back of my head that says, *What if you can't trust them? What if they will turn on you?* So you begin to tell them your story, the good and the bad parts. You start opening up about how you feel. You hush the worries that you'll be exposed by morning. You keep moving forward.

I learned that quantity can make me known. It can make me well liked. But I had quantity before the depression and it never made me full. It always left me wanting more. Like Jeff said, I had to go deep instead of wide. Quantity is all about the wide, and Quality is the one who takes you by the arm and says, "This won't be the easy route. It's not gonna be easy to go deeper with just a few. But aren't you ready for the layers to come off? Aren't you ready for someone to know you for who you really are? Just get ready, because feeling known is the best feeling in the world."

People don't stay. I used to believe the lie that investing wasn't worth it because people will leave you. Now I know the truth: you get over the fear of being left by becoming someone who stays.

I have one talk I deliver quite frequently when I get in front of an audience. It's called "Stay." The talk is divided into three main points: Stay hungry. Stay small. Stay here.

I never had an issue with being hungry. I've been hungry for something more my whole life. I never had an issue with being small. If anything, I play small too much of the time.

It's the "staying here" part that has always been my struggle. My friend Nia says loving someone—or allowing someone to love you—is hard because staying is hard. The two need each other to live. If you stay, you eventually have to let someone in. If you let someone in, you eventually have to drop the facade. If you stay, you eventually have to unpack your suitcases.

I've wondered for a while how to dismantle this lie we tell ourselves to not get invested because we are afraid to be left, and I've learned you need to do two things: let people into your mess and become a stayer too.

I think all of us should come with a warning label on the front of our packaging that reads, "If you love me long enough to stay with me, you will eventually see a side of me that I hate. It will be inevitable and it will be messy. I will break your heart. This is just one of the perks of being human."

I'm realizing this is one of the most common lies we believe. It's a lie that keeps us always at arm's length with other people because we think if we show too much, we'll be left behind. I don't know where the fear comes from, but I suspect all of us have felt the pain of being left.

131

I can't lie and say you won't ever be left. That's not true. People don't stay just because we want them to. But I can believe that one person leaving the narrative is not enough to shut out everyone else. There are people who stay. They stay, and they deserve medals for it.

In the months of my own recovery, I had a friend create beautiful stationery with the words "Thank You for Staying" etched on the front of them. I sent these cards to every person who walked with me through the dark and wasn't scared off by my mess.

I think that's how we quietly get over the fear of being left—we learn how to stick around for the people who need us. It reminds me of the story in the Bible about the good Samaritan. My pastor read it to us the other day, but he didn't focus on the points we usually take note of. Here's a story about a guy who gets beat up on the side of the road and left for dead. Two people pass him by before a third guy, the most unlikely of the three, stops to help the man.

My pastor said we look at this text and interpret this as the guy had stopped for a moment, but that's not the whole story. He stopped *for a while*. He took care of the man. He made the man his own priority for several days. That's hard for me to fathom. I think my first thought is, *Let's clean up the mess*. But here was a good guy who said, "It's going to be messy for a while, but I won't abandon you."

There's beauty in sticking with one another and seeing one another to the other side. If we wanted to, we could be the people who didn't just stick around for the good parts. We could be the type of people who stick around long enough for the story to change. There's redemption in staying to love others longer. It's louder than the fear of being left.

I'm alone. I used to believe the lie that I was all alone, left to fight my battles on my own. Now I know the truth: I am surrounded. I just need to be willing to reach out.

One of the best friends I've made in Atlanta is a guy named Jake. At the beginning of our friendship, Jake was saving up for a wedding ring when the girl whose finger he planned to place it on broke up with him. They'd been talking about engagement—and forever—for a while, but she ultimately felt like they weren't meant to last that long. Jake used the money he was saving up for that ring to buy a mattress instead.

Jake invited all his closest friends to a baseball game the night before his birthday. He was lively and excited. You would have never known he was probably spending most of his nights curled up in the fetal position, crying into his new mattress. It wasn't until the trip home from the game did he get quiet and somber.

"I just want to skip the day," he said. "You know what I mean? It's like, there's one person you want to hear from. And you know that person isn't going to call. You won't see their name pop up on your screen. I'd rather just skip it."

That evening, I devised a plan with two of Jake's closest friends. The following morning—the official day of Jake's birth—I sent out a tweet at 7 a.m. that read, "I'm looking for girls who are down for a secret mission. Email for details."

I expected to get twenty or thirty girls showing up in my inbox, waiting on the details for this "secret mission." I'd send each of them a template email I'd written about that day being Jake's birthday. I'd give them Jake's number and prompt them to call or text him to wish him a happy birthday. There was one rule—otherwise they could be as creative or outgoing as they wished: Don't tell Jake where you got the phone number. Make up a story and stick to it.

Emails started rolling in by 7:02 a.m. I spent that whole morning copying and pasting the template email back to dozens of girls interested in the mission.

Girls were emailing me back, sending screenshots of their interactions with Jake. They made up these elaborate stories. One claimed she and Jake met at Hogwarts. Another girl told Jake they met at a hoedown. They both stepped forward to do-si-do and switch partners and ended up dancing with one another. One girl drove to a bakery and took photos of all the different cakes in the window. "Which one do you want for today, Jake?" she asked.

A friend of ours who works with Jake stayed on watch the entire day. He said there wasn't a spare moment when Jake's phone wasn't buzzing. Jake was searching the internet to see if his phone number had accidentally been leaked online. He couldn't figure out where all the calls were coming from.

Throughout the day, more than three hundred girls got an email with Jake's phone number included in it.

At the end of the day, I called Jake to wish him a happy birthday and to apologize for accidentally giving his phone number to more than three hundred girls.

"I couldn't figure out what was going on!" he said. "I should have known it was you."

"I hope it wasn't too overwhelming for you," I told him.

"It was perfect," he said. "I was doing so good too. I was really enjoying all the texts and calls. I was holding it together and I didn't get sad throughout the entire day. And then I picked up one of the phone calls and heard an entire group of voices singing to me."

It turns out that one of the girls who emailed me taught sixth-grade biology. She included one of her classes in the secret mission and put the class on speakerphone as they sang happy birthday to Jake.

"That was the nail in my emotional coffin," Jake said. "All day, I just kept waiting to figure out if it was some joke. Like, 'Haha, Jake's phone number got plastered all over the internet and no one really cares.' They were singing to me and they said 'happy birthday, dear Jake.' When they said my name, I lost it. I just started weeping.

"That's the best feeling in the world, Hannah," he spoke again. "The feeling that someone knows your name."

The phone got quiet for a moment, but I didn't try to fill the space with words. We both sat there—on opposite ends of the line—silently with one another. The best feeling in the world is when someone knows your name.

I think that day will forever be one of my favorite days. I can't look at the span of seven hours I spent in the office and say I got any amount of work done. I don't think I did anything that day but send that template email out hundreds of times. Yet the impact of those emails was monumental. Some days aren't about what you get done; they're about who you empower.

If I ever doubted people on the internet, I don't anymore. There's the occasional troll you wish someone would ban from all forms of social media, but for the most part, there are a lot of decent and hungry people behind the screen. They're waiting to do something that matters, something that counts. I think we are all a little hungry to do something that matters.

I learned that afternoon that so many of us are fighting an unseen battle. Because the work we are doing is so internal, there's pressure to give up. There's the lie that wants us to believe we are all alone—isolated and never coming back from it.

For that one day, I put myself and all my worries on the back burner and showed up to help other people surround Jake with love. That's when I realized I wasn't alone. When you show up to help someone else get through the day, you begin to see we're all in the battle. We are all just trying to make it through this life somewhat triumphantly. We may get lonely at some points, but we are never actually alone.

So I guess I know the next step in this journey to beat out the lies, to find a way to clear out the camp. Any path toward change will lead you to the camps in your brain where the liars build fires and tell ghost stories at night. You have to be willing to work out the lies. You have to become someone who fights the lies with something more powerful—truth.

Anne Lamott writes, "Lies cannot nourish or protect you. Only freedom from fear, freedom from lies, can make us beautiful, and keep us safe."[1] Lies are like rumors. Believe the rumor for long enough, and eventually it will become truth to you. You will start believing it without even realizing it. The only way to really dispel a rumor is to figure out the truth and go to the source.

I wish I could just mail you the magic bullet to fat burning and mind renewal, all packed into one pill, but it doesn't work that way. The only way I've ever learned to tackle the lies is to battle with truth. To battle with truth, you need to learn truth.

---

1. Anne Lamott, *Grace (Eventually): Thoughts on Faith* (New York: Riverhead, 2007), 74.

It makes me think about David and all the psalms he wrote. There are days where I feel like David is being dramatic or maybe oversharing, but I must remind myself that David was under a lot of pressure and had physical enemies surrounding him frequently.

Psalm 42 is one of my favorites because David asks the famous question, "Why, my soul, are you downcast?" It wasn't until recently that I realized David is calling out those voices we let in and allow to speak over our lives. You know the ones. They tell us we can't make a difference. They tell us we are not worthy. They are the harassing voices that tell us to just give up. But David is genius for waking up, looking around, and saying, "Wait . . . I have more power than I think. I don't have to be governed by this voice. I am going back to putting my hope in God."

I cling to this belief that God isn't some flippant coach who is waiting for us to fail. He isn't shifty. He does not whisper riddles in dark corners. He doesn't try to confuse us. I remember asking for prayer during one of those hard days in my depression, and my friend Andrew led the prayer. He placed his hand on my head at one point and said, "You know his voice, Hannah. You know this is not his voice." But it is so easy to forget. It's easy to forget what he sounds like when the lies are so loud.

It would break my heart to stand in God's shoes and witness his kids constantly picking these unkind voices and believing it's the best version of God they'll ever get. There's so much more for us, but we need to be willing to locate the lies.

There are multiple times throughout any given month when I will stop what I am doing, pull out a piece of paper, and write down every lie I am believing in my brain. I learned how to do this in my depression. My friends had me sit down and track the lies. Once the lie is on paper, it loses a little bit of its power. In a way, you've caught it. You've shined a flashlight on it, and it cannot maneuver itself off the page.

Scientists say that once you write down a thought, it becomes malleable. You become able to change it. So once all my lies are written down, I begin crossing them out one by one and start writing the truth in its place. Sometimes the truth is Scripture. Sometimes the truth is something a person I love said about me. A lot of times I know the truth. It is just waiting for me to reach out and use it.

The exercise of writing truths and crossing out lies is powerful. Try it. Brooke and I make whole evenings out of it. We will get together, make some dinner, and then write down our truths and lies. We take turns telling each other how ridiculous the lies are, and it feels nice to not stand inside your brain alone.

Together, we rewire pathways in our brains. I know it sounds crazy, but that's actually what happens when we start evicting certain lies and finding better, more truthful tenants. There's a verse in the Bible everyone overuses and says so flippantly we tend to not even take it seriously: "Do not conform . . . but be transformed by the renewing of your mind" (Romans 12:2). That verse is meant to be a challenge. It's not meant to be an overnight fix. A lot of times, renewing your mind looks like sitting at the kitchen table and writing down verses about love until they seep into you, until they start telling different stories in your brain to trump the fear. It's a process—a long and arduous process—but one you can trust.

STEAL THIS PRAYER

Dear God, I need to see the lies in black-and-white. Strip out their fake and concentrated colors and amplify the lies in black-and-white so I can do the work of uprooting them. Where are the weeds in my life? Show me. I want to be faithful. I want to be alive and fully awake to all good things you're doing around me.

STEAL THIS PRAYER

| Chapter Twelve | **BE THE INVITATION** |

When the internet first became a thing, I was obsessed with chat rooms. I'd come home after school and log on to talk to all my "friends" in the teenage chat room of AOL. It was there that I met BomberRon89, the star of my first great love story. BomberRon and I never met. We never exchanged pictures. We didn't talk on the phone. Through a series of instant messages, I got to know him, and it was enough for me to think we would one day meet and get married. We said "I love you," like thirteen-year-olds do. And then one day, with no warning, BomberRon was gone. His screen name was deleted, and I never heard from him again. Still, to this day, I go to places like the mall or the airport and find myself thinking, *Maybe that's him . . . Maybe that's BomberRon.*

I understand that BomberRon could very well have been a thirty-nine-year-old man. I'll likely never know. This is not an exemplary story. Rather, it's a story about the power of screens. Even though I was only thirteen, there was something desirable about a person I only had to talk to through a screen. You share what you want to share. You duck out when you want to duck out. It's both convenient and noncommittal to hold someone at a distance while always putting your best self forward through calculated messages and witty internet banter.

I understand why a lot of people fall in love on the internet without even knowing a person, and I can also empathize with the people who hide behind a fake profile because they're afraid they will not be loved for who they really are. To an extent, I think that's all of us. We want to be loved, really loved, but we struggle to figure out what that looks like. We are afraid that if we are real with people, they will leave us. They will deem us to be flawed or too messed up to stick with. We want to find people who see all our imperfections and decide to choose us anyway, but there's risk in that. Giving people this perfect perception of you and then running away is always easier than staying until they see your real junk.

Recently, I was talking with the director of a company in Atlanta, having a conversation over churros about the importance of "community." I wish all tough life conversations could happen over Mexican desserts. There are definitely more resolutions when carbs are involved.

He was telling me there honestly aren't many days where he doesn't think about leaving, about quitting his job to go do something simpler.

"I never get too far with those thoughts though," he said, grabbing another churro from the basket. "When I remember there is a team of twenty-five people behind me, I know I can't leave. I think about my people, and then I don't think about leaving any longer."

His words stuck with me long after the guilt from eating so many churros faded from my conscience. I love that he was confident enough to say, "my people"—as in people I can claim as my own, people I stick up for, people I go to bat for, people I lay myself on the line for. I think the most precious thing I'll ever get to say in this lifetime is that I found "my people."

I wish, though, that it was simpler to find people who want to see you win. I wish relationships operated swiftly, the way they do in an episode of *Friends*, where you always know if you show up at the coffee shop, someone will meet you there.

For a long time, I surrounded myself with people who didn't really care if I won. To be honest, we were a shallow group. We gossiped a lot. We found strength in putting other people down. I walked through several years of college with these girls, and I acted no better than them. I found out if we weren't talking about someone, we didn't have much to talk about at all. I would have picked different community for myself back then if it had been possible, but I honestly don't think I would have known what to look for. Knowing what you want and need in a community isn't as easy as picking it out on Amazon and waiting two days for it to show up. You must ask yourself tough questions to figure out who you're supposed to hang around with:

- Who do I want to be a year from now?
- What hurdles do I want to overcome?
- What am I good at, and how do I bring that into relationships?
- How do I take care of people?
- What do I value in myself and other people?

These are just a few questions that won't lend themselves to perfect community. No community is perfect. I think it's easier to move toward something different than what you've always done when you get honest with yourself.

My first month rooted in Atlanta after I resolved to stay and build a life there, Jake invited me to have dinner with a few of his closest friends, people he'd just started hanging out with and suddenly was incredibly close with. I wondered at first if they were a cult. But when I met these people for the first time—three ordinary people trying to do something unordinary with their friend group—I immediately wanted it. I wanted what they had because I could tell that no one at the table was faking it.

We talked honestly about how we felt that the word *community* had been watered down—with lots of thanks to social media. We throw the word around and then wonder if we're the only person asking, "Am I missing something?" Because this doesn't feel like real community; it feels like a Coke commercial. It just feels like I'm stalking someone's social media feeds hoping to get the invite.

It's easy to slip into a pattern where you don't really take care of your relationships. Investing in someone's life is not the same as investigating someone's life. One requires patience, capacity, and continuing to be there when the door looks so enticing. We cannot be people who accept a check-in text or a comment on a photo as enough to say we are truly living in community.

All five of us had done our share of asking the tough questions: Is community even real? Is it possible? Do people actually show up at two in the morning? How do you choose to stay when you'd rather bolt for the door?

Jake tells me that when you continuously show up for other people and give yourself to the world around you, people will want to do life with you. "Authentic community is a product of character," he says. When you work on yourself, you'll find other people trying to do the same thing.

For the next few months, we dug in and really started building a community in Atlanta. I don't think I could have ever found this kind of community until I committed to sticking around. We prayed about our little group of people and asked God to open the doors for more to come in. We loaned each other money. We made dinners for one another and had slumber parties for each other's birthdays. We vetted potential mates. We ate a ton of cheesy quinoa (like, too much cheesy quinoa). We pushed one another to get offline and get deeper with God when things were tough. We experienced pain and loss beside one another, joy and grief. Our group of six morphed into a group of eleven because people fell in love, got married, and more people naturally came in. We kept coming to the table, over and over again, and it was beautiful. We had the most remarkable experience putting each other first.

One of my favorite moments was Easter Sunday when we decided to share a "breakfast for dinner" after church. For many of us, it was our first Easter away from home. I will forever remember that night, all of us packed around a table and laughing harder than we'd ever laughed before.

At one point, Jake took a picture and posted it to social media. Several of us reposted it at the end of the night because it was the best depiction of our Easter Sunday. A bunch of us are laughing. A few more are talking in intimate circles. There is bacon on the table. We are celebrating and nothing is fake. For a fleeting four-hour breakfast, there was nothing wrong with the world. We were certain we could handle whatever life decided to throw at us next.

Someone commented on Jake's photo, "I'm coming." To this day, Jake talks about that comment and how it's his favorite thing he's ever seen on social media. Just the words "I'm coming," which meant we were creating a space for the community we all desired, and more people were coming to join us.

I think every one of us wants an invitation to sit at a table like that. For years I thought, *This should be happening more easily.*

We need community, but it doesn't shape itself overnight. The building of it takes time, failure, and vulnerability. We have to put ourselves out there, being honest in front of other people, and we won't always be met there in the middle—but sometimes it will happen. When it happens, it's beautiful. Social media wants us to believe that one party will mend our little hearts and fill in the holes that ache for meaningful interactions, but we all have to work more than that. It is work to show up to the places where we meet other people. And it is work to open up our hearts after we closed up shop for a little while.

So look for the people who understand you. Don't stop until you find them. And when you find them, take care of them. Always keep thanking them. Always keep them close. Let them buy plane tickets to see you. Let them talk crazy. Let them go. When they need to go out there in the world and see what it has for them, let them go. Commit their birthdays to memory. Show up with soup. Celebrate them on their biggest and worst days. Keep an open invitation always on the table that simply says, *You are welcome on my couch, you and all your issues, at any time.* Push them. Spur them on. Believe in them on the day they come to you and whisper, "I don't know what I want."

Be real with them. Scary real. Real friendship cannot be fake. It will kill our souls if we walk around acting like we are cheering for people when we really aren't. At the heart of what we do for one another, there must be love. The other stuff will break us apart eventually. Love is the only thing that holds, and it must call us deeper than what we thought we were capable of giving.

My friend Brett recently wrote in a Facebook post, "Christian people believe that God is the light of the soul. We also believe that humans are created in the *imago Dei*, the image of God. That means we bear a little of that divine light just by being human. This is why human connection is so powerful. Humans are better together, especially when we are living in community. People bring that light."

I don't mean we need to be living in the same neighborhood or the same building. I also don't think it's wrong to have multiple groups of people you hang out with and live life with. I think letting people see you and really know you is what allows you to distinguish the lies that have tried to hold you back. Good people, the ones who are really in your corner, will help you stop telling old stories and start building new ones.

In the group, I found myself getting really close to Dawn. There's something about Dawn that makes me want to be a better human. She is a challenge to me in that way. I am reminded of it every time I open the Bible to read the words of Jesus and he is constantly talking about "good deeds." Not good words, not good "maybe I will do that soon," but good deeds. Good action steps.

Dawn reaches out to me frequently to make plans. Every week, I can count on getting a message from her seeking to hang out. Dawn isn't interested in being the best friend to every single person in the room. She models friendship by staying committed, consistent, and concerned.

There aren't too many people you can be scary honest with and still have them be there at the end of the day. But I think this is real friendship: not being afraid to lose it all in front of another person because you know you will still be loved.

I think the right kind of community will show you who you are and where you can go with a kinder voice than the one you talk to yourself with. Community happens when we show up for it and keep showing up for it even after the shininess wears off. It opens us up.

I get stuck a lot in this perpetual worry that everyone in my life is hanging out without me. It sucks away my joy. It dictates my emotions. I want the invitations. Even if I cannot attend, and even if these are not the people I need to be surrounded by, I still want the invite.

One of my older friends tells me I need to be the invitation. She tells me that if I'm constantly worried about not getting an invitation from people in our neighborhood to hang or clink glasses or celebrate a birthday, then I should put my big girl pants on and just be the invitation.

In practical terms, she's telling me to invite people in. Invite people to the table. I listen to my friend and decide to be an invitation. I noticed there was one thing that all my girl-friends talked about when we gathered to watch *The Bachelor* on Monday night: fitness. Every girl in that room wanted to become healthier and happier. Fitness, for me, is a long-lost love. When I was in college, I spent hours poring over wellness books. I taught myself how to use all the heavy weights at the gym. I feel empowered and strong when I lift weights. I want others to feel that too. So I issued the invitation.

I created a workout group to meet three days a week at

7 a.m. Together, we lunged, squatted, ran, and lifted weights. We laughed, listened to nineties playlists, sweat, and planked. It became the thing I looked most forward to as the group grew larger.

People want to get the invite as much as I do. Instead of worrying about missing out, I remind myself to continually just be that invite. I'm learning it's that simple. You can create an event. You can host a movie night. You don't have to worry about everyone in the room knowing one another. People don't have to become best friends by the end of it. Just say one big prayer over the whole shindig: that hearts will connect, that prayers will be answered, phone numbers will be swapped, and the community will grow in a way you can't possibly take credit for.

STEAL THIS PRAYER

Dear God, I know I cannot do this life alone. Surround me with people who want good for my life, people who will challenge me to another level. Help me to build others up and be an encourager during hard times. Keep me centered on selflessness, kindness, and honesty in all of my interactions. Let my relationships always point back to you.

Chapter Thirteen | FIND THE CHURCH

My quest to find church began with a piece of avocado toast.

On this particular morning, I took a picture of said toast. I placed it on a white plate, took it into my bedroom where the natural light floods perfectly through the windows, set the plate on a yellow blanket, and snapped a photo. Of toast.

I cropped and filtered the photo of toast. I added contrast and a little bit of brightness to my toast picture. I prepared my toast to show herself to the world. This was my toast's best life now.

I transferred my photo of toast into Instagram and prepared to write my caption. I would say something about the drizzled honey or the Himalayan sea salt sprinkled over it. I would gush about the organic avocado that is spread evenly—in delightful chunks of green goodness—across the twenty-seven-grain (or whatever) Ezekiel bread.

I said, "Little Toast, are you ready for your finest moment?" Little Toast in that very moment could not have been readier to meet the approval of others who wished they had eaten breakfast or had resisted the drive-thru or were also enjoying avocado toast on a rainy morning when they had an extra thirty minutes to brew their coffee like a barista.

But when it came to Little Toast, there was nothing for me to say. I realized in that moment, sitting on a yellow blanket spread on my bed across from the uneaten little toast, that it was pointless to write anything about toast. It wouldn't change anyone. A photo of toast would not make the life of a single person better.

I'd spent the morning reading a few chapters in the book of Acts. In Acts, the first church is born. I used to tiptoe around Acts because I found the word *church* to be too messy to deal with. Sitting in that blank caption space, ready to write about toast, all I could think about was the church.

Right at the beginning of Acts (2:42), the first church is described. It says these people devoted themselves to teaching, fellowship with one another, the breaking of bread, and prayer. They ate a lot of carbs together. They were so devoted to one another that they started selling off their possessions in the hope that they could lift one another up with their monetary returns. They attended the temple together. They were thankful when they got to eat. They were always saying thanks to God, and people really liked them. And because of all this, the Lord multiplied them. More and more people were praying, living life, and eating toast together. Seems like a pretty beautiful life to me.

It's likely the first church didn't document their toast. Talking about their lives through documentation wasn't a priority to them; people were. They wanted to love people so well—so deep and so wide—that eventually their own self-obsession would get swallowed up by a bigger story. I think it's a million times harder to get to that place today because our culture measures us constantly. It sizes us up. It tells us we need to have followers. It tells us to keep chasing. Just keep chasing the next best thing.

I don't think that first church was perfect. I know it wasn't.

I'm certain the people had baggage back then, just like we've got it now. There were definitely the angry and the crazy ex-girlfriends and the humble-braggers, even if they didn't have Facebook to play it all out on. All churches and people groups have those. But the church was the first pair of open arms. That's what I take away from Acts 2:42. The church was always meant to be the first pair of open arms. How did we get away from this simple and organic idea of church? How did church become this massive, sprawling thing that can feel so high-tech and complicated?

_____

From my earliest memories, up until after college, church was a place where I didn't belong. I didn't feel seen. I didn't feel like God was actually mighty or real in this place. I felt like I was going to watch the girls around me get married young to good men and I'd be left behind. I felt like God had blessings for others but not for me.

I wouldn't have told you it was a safe place where I ate carbs with friends and sold my things because I loved them so much and actually wanted to worship alongside them. That may have been the first church, but it wasn't my church reality.

I attended church only to make my mom happy. I had no attachment to the building or the people, and about 70 percent of the church was over the age of forty. My longest span of consecutive church attendance happened when people thought I should date the cute, shy bass player in the church band. That weekly church ritual ended shortly after he took me on a date. As we were driving to the beach and getting out of the car, he made a joke that he had black trash bags in the trunk in case he needed to chop me into bits and get rid of the body. I learned that night that guys who play the bass at church are not required to be holy. Some churches will give any dude a guitar and teach him how to raise his hands between notes.

In all of my church attendance at a young age, I was just looking for something real. Statistics say that young people are leaving the church at a more rapid rate than ever. I think it's because we've adjusted to a feeble diet of fake and filtered things for so long that we can't help but ache for something real. Richard Foster writes, "The desperate need today is not for a greater number of intelligent people, or gifted people, but for deep people."[1] He wrote those words in the 1970s, and I keep thinking to myself, *How much more relevant are the words today? How much hungrier are we for something real?* Something more than staged toast.

I think people want depth when it comes to church. Eventually, the productions of a church wear off and it comes down to one question: Can I meet with God here? Will these people bring me closer to the real God or push me further away? Your answer will likely determine whether you stay or go. Whether you plant roots or reach for your suitcase again.

As I was building an everyday sort of life in Georgia, a friend of mine asked if I would be willing to help out someone they knew by taking a survey on the church in the Western world. She was compiling data from people across Atlanta, and I agreed to participate.

---

1. Richard Foster, *Celebration of Discipline: The Path to Spiritual Growth* (San Francisco: HarperSanFrancisco, 1978), 1.

She and I met in my favorite coffee shop. We sat off in the corner, and she handed me earbuds with a microphone attached. Her questions were neutral at first, but then they became intrusive and pointed. I didn't have nearly the number of answers about the church that I thought I would have.

I'm sure the individual conducting the survey meant well, but the questions asked were invasive. They carried an agenda that I could not quite put my finger on. I felt really violated as she asked me questions about personal sins and who I did or did not think would go to heaven, as if I had some invite list. There were so many moments in the span of that interview when I wanted to take off the headphones and walk away. I wasn't brave enough though.

When it was over, I quickly exited the coffee shop, got into my car, and burst into tears. I remember saying, "What the heck?" over and over again to God in the car.

Author Anne Lamott believes there are three essential prayers: Help, Thanks, and Wow.[2] I would add one more: What the heck?

"Why?" Better yet, "I can't even."

I feel like I could pray the "I can't even" prayer seven times before dinner.

There are so many instances in the world today that call for the "What the heck?" prayer to be used, to scream up toward God, "I don't get it. I don't understand it. I don't know what the point is. The point of this pain. The point of our ignorance. The news we watch. The cruel things we do. I can't even, sweet Jesus. What the heck do you want me to do?"

---

2. Anne Lamott, *Help, Thanks, Wow: The Three Essential Prayers* (New York: Riverhead, 2012).

I was angry and then suddenly brokenhearted for all the people in the world trying to find God but meeting people who make them feel violated, broken, and not good enough. I think that's why some people avoid the church—they're afraid they will walk into the building and be too much for God. Too much for people.

We mistake what is happening in the news as the church. We mistake people kicking us down or telling us we are "too much" for God as the church. This stuff isn't church. Church is our meeting in the questions. Church is us acknowledging that God is bigger than our questions, that his love is greater than our insecurities or our impatience with one another. I think church only happens when we get smaller so the love of God can get bigger.

I already told you about how I attend the "Church of *The Bachelor*" on Monday nights. I mean that in a completely not-sacrilegious way. After I stopped running from the people who wanted to get to know me, I found myself becoming a more open person. And something started happening within our little group of girls.

There was one *Bachelor* night when the living room had a depressing weight to it. One girl had lost her aunt the week prior. Two of us were going through breakups. Another girl was waiting on the results of tests to determine whether her mother had cancer.

On this particular night, we were a bundle of questions. Everyone just wanted to talk and no one was watching the episode that night. At some point, one of the girls paused the episode completely and we just started opening up about what frustrated us, what was hurting us, what didn't make sense in the moment.

The thing is, most of us go to different churches. Some of us don't go to church. Others don't even believe in God. And yet we all had this silly dramatic show as a common thread that put us in that room that night.

We broke off into pockets. Five of us ended up in the other room sitting on the kitchen floor. One of the girls pulled out her phone and began reading Isaiah 61 out loud by the glow of the screen. Her voice was tired and trembling. We started to pray.

The moment was holy. I looked around the room and realized that this thing we were doing, was church. In a world that drives us to our knees with all the chaos in it, I am a believer that you can invite God anywhere. Some people get too legalistic with God's whereabouts. The God of the people is everywhere though. There's no space too dark that he can't poke a hole into it and let some light stream in. God can and will meet you on the kitchen floor.

I am a regular attendee of the "Church of the Kitchen Floor." Admittedly, I sometimes sit there more than I sit in pews. But what I love about the Bible is that Jesus never says, "In order to make church happen, you need a big building and you need a band." No, church is where the brokenhearted meet the homeless. Church is where the ones who pretend to have it all together intersect with the ones who openly admit, "I do *not* have this all together. Not even close." Church happens when we cease molding perfect images of ourselves and just look up. We help one another look up in the hope that, together, we will find something perfect.

I picked a church when I decided to stay in Atlanta. *Go there every Sunday. Make it your home.* That's what I told myself I needed to do: *just pick one and invest.*

In the South, there are almost too many options for church. The longer I battled with indecision about the church, the more I found myself falling into an ugly pattern of comparing churches. I've sat at too many brunch tables to count, listening to people rehash the church fails they've experienced.

I realized I'm not helping any church when I contribute to these conversations, so I've tried to stop. I think about past boyfriends and how, when we didn't work out, I'd feel so much power in gossiping about them to my friends. It made me feel victorious—like I had the upper hand—when I could talk about all the reasons we weren't right for one another and he was the one who had insurmountable issues. I see now that talking about the other person never made me any happier; it actually made me sadder. It hurt more to know they were doing just fine. It stung when they fell in love with the right person before I did. I eventually had to stop gossiping about my exes and start praying for them.

These were not enthusiastic prayers. They were simple and quick—whenever one of my exes popped into my brain and I had the option of attacking them with my words. Instead of hanging my thoughts on their shortcomings, I've prayed they would get better in that area. I have prayed that the area I saw as their weakest point would become their greatest strength. I have done my best to choose prayer over patronizing. I am finding that my heart is lighter. Now I'm doing the same thing for churches.

I once had an older gentleman I looked up to say to me

you can never take a person at 80 percent with the hope that the other 20 percent will change. If you go into a relationship that way, you'll spend all your best energy trying to change him or her. He said you had to be willing to take a person at 100 percent. You must be willing to say, "I will choose you for who you are, not for who I am dependent on you becoming." I think it is the same for churches. You choose a church, embrace the flaws and the messiness of it, and call it home.

I'm not saying churches don't mess up in massive ways. We all do. We all get it wrong sometimes. I just realized for myself that I needed to stop waiting for my church to mess up and fail me. I needed to start participating rather than poke holes in the foundation. I found God in church when I stopped showing up to find flaws in the people.

Glennon Doyle writes, "Church is a group of folks working their stuff out together, gently. There is no shortcut to church. It's slow, and it's real life, and you have to show up for it."[3]

I began showing up. I decided to get involved. I joined the hospitality team. I was simply in charge of making coffee and feeding people bagels. It was glorious. I joined a prayer team and learned just how much prayer goes into every event the church hosts.

I became more committed to the college group at my church, and I'm pretty thankful that I didn't get the chance to go onstage with a microphone that first month, or even that first year. Maybe I'd done a few impressive things that made me feel entitled to that sort of attention, but I have to believe God knew that wasn't for me in this place. That wasn't why I was there. I was there to fill up water jugs and refill coffee stations. I was there to repaint

---

3. Glennon Doyle, "My Church," *Momastery*, December 22, 2013, http://momastery.com/blog/2013/12/22/6664.

rooms and drive people to service projects. I was there to pray with someone who didn't know how to pray or to buy a backpack for a child who didn't have the luxury of going to Target at the beginning of the school year. It was all a bunch of basic action steps that challenged me to step outside of myself. When I step outside of myself, I see God. I help others see him too.

I feel like I should warn you about what's going to happen though. It happened to me, and so it will likely happen to you. You'll get bored. I can almost promise you this. You will go through seasons when you don't want to show up to church and you don't feel like singing. You will experience these droughts in your faith that will make you want to stop investing. I think the bravest thing you can do in that moment when you feel like giving up on the church is to keep going back. Go back when it is ordinary. Go back when it is monotonous. Go back when you are tired of the role you are in. There—in the going back—the magic will happen.

I realize, with every step I take toward involvement, that church isn't some building where I go to sing songs or pray extra prayers. Church is a thing I participate in. Church happens when we show up and God gets to move in and through the ways we love and care for one another.

It makes me think of an email I got the other week from two girls who are starting a group on Monday nights where they'll sit with people at their college, eat with them, and basically have an honesty hour once a week. Their plan is to devour breakfast food while talking about real stuff together. Bacon and bruises from where life hits hardest. I really dig their plan. They want to be Jesus to people, and they realize Jesus had infinite capacity to sit and dine with jacked-up people.

To me, these girls are the first church. They get it. They are craving real life off the screen. They are invested in the idea of friendship, and real conversation, carbs, and the building of a safe place where anyone can come in and say, "Hey, I've got this darkness. Can you help me clear it out for good?" That's the only way church works—in a building or in a home: if we are willing to put down our guards, our fears, our things that make us afraid to be different, and meet one another.

They realize they are one piece—one piece that needs to do its part in loving others, communing, asking tough stuff, and singing back to God with robust songs of gratitude. To them, it's not about crafting an experience that will leave others out; it's about something real.

I think that's truly what Jesus wanted when church became a thing. I think he always wanted the church to act as invitation, a place to go to wrestle through faith together. We are all invited to do the work.

The Jesus I read about had one simple question and then one command to follow it.

"Do you love me?"

He asked that question three times to Simon Peter (John 21:15–19).

"Do you love me?"

Not, "are you perfect?" Not, "do you never sin?" Not, "are you holding your life together?" Perfection was never God's prerequisite. I have to believe he knew exactly who he was asking for when he reached down to us.

"Do you love me?"

And if you love me—if your answer is yes—then feed my sheep. That was his command: feed my sheep.

I translate "feed my sheep" into a lot of different action steps: Show up for my people. Stand at the door and welcome them in. Listen to their stories. Stay attentive. Give until it hurts. Stay in the mess with people. Dig in the deep end. Walk in shoes that make you uncomfortable. Speak hard truths. Ask hard questions.

Feed my sheep. Stay up through the night. Get them breakfast. Meet them at diners. Sit in their uncertainty. Give them your shoulders and your tired arms.

Stay up. Wait for people to come home. Just wait. Be a light that is still on when they finally come home. I like to imagine a church where the doors are unlocked and the sign is always glowing bright and reading, OPEN.

These are dark and confusing times. I think we're all a little lost and searching for light. I think we're all just wondering if someone will leave the light on for us. If they will leave the door open. If they will usher us in, saying, "Come to the table and eat. You must be hungry. Here, let's eat." It's the company, the belonging, that we're most hungry for. The bacon is just the bonus.

STEAL THIS PRAYER

Dear God, strip down the bones of church for me and make me see where I need to decrease and you need to grow. God, change this heart of mine to want real community more than I want followers. Bring me people to eat with, laugh with, mourn with, and stand with when injustice is roaring. God, give me something real to call your church apart from a filtered photo and a standard I've never been able to stand inside of.

Chapter Fourteen

DON'T FLUSH THE FISH

The other day, I got an email from a reader who is about to turn twenty-six. In the spirit of preparing for another year of life, she decided to reach out to twenty-six people and ask for wisdom about the twenty-sixth year. I maybe wasn't the best person to ask for this wisdom. I was never so happy to see twenty-six finally leave me alone. Twenty-six was like a relative you invite into your home for too long of a time. On the day they're flying home, you get them to the airport three hours early and don't look back in the rearview mirror as you drive off, leaving them by the curbside with their suitcase.

I only see twenty-six in its fullness because of twenty-seven.

On my twenty-seventh birthday (which was really just a going-away party for twenty-six), I'd never felt so loved before. It was three months after I moved back to Atlanta for good, but I felt that, at this point, I'd been out of the woods for the last month. I planned my own birthday at a hole-in-the-wall taco joint called Holy Taco. My friends and I filled four tables shaped in an L. I looked around the tables on several occasions and found myself in awe of the life I'd built this past year. One of my friends gave me a key with the word "KNOWN" engraved into the metal. That is the best way to describe how I felt that night: surrounded and known. I think feeling known is synonymous with feeling loved. The two play off of one another to make a perfect combination. If someone can know all the different parts of you—see you at your best and at your weakest—and still love you, that's the gold of life. That's what we came here for.

In the center of the table, between big bowls of queso and guacamole, sat a beta fish in a fishbowl with a map of the world etched on the glass with white frost. My friend Jenna got me the fish and named it after my favorite rapper, Childish Gambino. Child"fish" Gambino lived a triumphant nine months before being brutally murdered by my roommate's cat in a freak accident in which the mirror on my vanity toppled over, smashing Childish's bowl into a million pieces and leaving him paralyzed for twenty-four hours before we let him go.

I started dating a guy named Daniel the week of that birthday. Last minute, I decided to invite him to the party, so he was there the whole evening sitting right beside me. I liked how, even though we didn't really know each other, he rested his hand on my knee as I told stories.

After the party, Daniel asked if I want to grab a drink before heading home. I said yes, but we never got that drink. Instead, we drove around the highways of Atlanta.

"I didn't plan to take you for a drink," he said. "I just wanted to show you the city at night."

He told me there's a spot on the highway that if you go under the bridge, you can see the whole skyline of Atlanta unfold in front of you. That's where he wanted to take me. The car was eerily quiet as we moved toward the on-ramp. "You can put some music on," I said.

"A song is coming," he said. "I've got it queued up. I'm waiting for just the right moment."

We entered the interstate.

"You know how you said earlier that there are some things in life you just can't find the words for?" he asked.

I nodded.

"This is one of those moments."

As he said this, his finger clicked Play on his iPhone. A song streamed through the speakers of his old car as we drove beneath the bridge and up through the underpass. The lights of Atlanta met us, showing off in an impressive display. He reached for my hand. I held the fish in my other arm.

The next morning, I wake up and call my mom in a panic.

"Mom," I say, "Jenna got me a fish."

"A fish? Doesn't she know you hate fish?"

"When would that ever come up? I don't just tell people I'm afraid of fish."

I've been afraid of fish since I was a little girl. Not fish in the sea or the ocean. For some reason, I have some strange aversion to pet fish. I can't even walk into a pet store because the sight of multiple fish (never mind hundreds of them) will make me break out in hives.

"I don't know what to do with it," I tell her. "I can't even look at it."

"Where is the fish?"

"It's in the guest bedroom. I put it in there because I was too afraid to wake up and see it in the morning."

"You have to go get the fish and bring it back to the pet store."

"But I want to like the fish. Maybe I can like the fish."

"Well, that fish is going to suffer while you try to get over the fear."

I loved the idea of having a fish the night before. It seemed like the perfect birthday gift when it was sitting on the table at Holy Taco, swimming happily without a care in the world. But now the fish is mine and I am alone with it and I am responsible for its health and well-being.

"I need you to come over and help me flush this fish down the toilet," I tell Daniel over the phone that night.

"Wait, what? You want me to help you kill a fish? You loved the fish last night. You couldn't stop talking about the fish."

"I know. But that was last night. And last night I was at a party. I didn't have to be alone with the fish. I didn't have to take care of the fish."

"So you don't like the responsibility that comes with the fish, then . . ." He's trying to pull something more out of me.

"I don't like the fish. Period. This was a bad idea, and I need you to come over and flush it."

We argue back and forth over whether he'll help me flush my day-old fish down the toilet. This is a typical argument for two people who've been dating, sort of, for three days.

"Okay, I'll come over and flush it." He eventually gives in.

"Just so you know, I'm not flushing the fish."

It's the first thing Daniel says when he enters the house a half hour later.

"But you told me you would. That's why you came over."

"No," he says, "that's not why I came over. I would never actually agree to your plan of killing the fish. That's just cruel. It doesn't make any sense."

"Then why you are here?" I am not amused.

"I came over to take the fish from you," he continues. "I'm going to take the fish to my house for a few days. And then, when you're ready, you're going to tell me you want the fish back. You're going to get over this fear and you're going to take the fish back."

Daniel rescues Childish from the guest bedroom where he'd been locked up in the dark since the night before and places his bowl on the kitchen countertop. We stare at the fish for a while as it swims and taunts me from behind the glass.

"So what's the real story here?" he asks.

"What do you mean?"

"Like, you're not actually afraid of a fish," he says, moving the fishbowl to the side and taking a seat on the countertop. He motions for me to sit beside him. "What's really going on?"

"I don't know," I say. "I guess I just don't want to take care of it if it's just going to die in a few weeks anyway. Fish never last."

"So that's what you are afraid of? You're afraid that good things don't last?"

That's always been the bigger fear inside me wearing different hats: Good things don't last. People don't stay. Love doesn't win. I don't like the thought of building something when you don't know how long it will last. I once loved a boy so hard that I knew every detail of him. And when it was over, I didn't know what to do with all the pieces of him. Breaking up was like slowly writing a dictionary with someone and then realizing you could no longer use any of the words you still loved. I think I built up walls after that. I think each year and relationship were more layers of concrete on the walls.

I'm continually surprised by how present fear is in my life. When I think I've overcome a hurdle, another shows up that seems bigger and more impossible to get over. Apparently God even uses beta fish with a life expectancy of two weeks to make us face what scares us.

"I guess so. I think about waking up one day and seeing the fish dead. I don't want it to die on my watch."

"But fish die all the time."

"Yeah, but I don't want to invest in something if it's just going to die," I admit. "I just don't like investing in things if I know I'm going to lose in the end."

I knew it was about more than just a fish.

I'm not actually afraid of a dumb fish. I am afraid because the fish belongs to me. It is mine, and I must take care of it. If the fish is a bigger metaphor for the life I've built in the last few months, here's what I am really grappling with: I don't like fully leaning into a life where I don't control the outcome, when the characters come and go, and who makes it in the end. I cannot script dialogue for people or keep them if I want to. I am scared of losing them, of losing all I've built, because for maybe the first time I'm in love with the outcome. I want every little piece of my life.

We sit on the countertop late into the night talking about the importance of staying. We stop in fragments to wave at the fish and coo at it. It is Daniel's best effort to help me get over this fear. Around 1 a.m., I walk Daniel and the fish out to his car. We seat belt the bowl into the front seat.

"Drive slow," I say. "It would be traumatizing if the fish fell out of the bowl while you were driving."

"Okay," he says, closing the passenger door.

"Hey, Hannah . . ."

"Yeah?"

"I'm going to hug you now."

"Okay . . . ." I say, skeptical over why he is telling me this.

"I'm going to hug you and you can hold on for as long as you want to. But I'm not going anywhere and I just want you to know that."

He takes me into his arms in the middle of the road. We don't move. We don't say anything because words mess these moments up. We stand there, and he doesn't let go of me.

Eventually he speaks. "Hey, Hannah," he whispers into my ear.

"Yes?"

"Don't flush me."

"Don't flush you?"

"Yeah, like the fish. Don't flush me before you know where this is going. I can tell you over and over again that I'm not going anywhere, but it won't make a difference if you decide to flush me. I don't have control over that. So just don't flush me yet."

A few minutes later, I watch him drive off with my fish. I stand on the porch, not wanting to go inside yet. I feel raw and vulnerable, as if I have been wearing a mask up until the point where Daniel asked me to take it off so he could see what was actually there. He called the fear inside me by name, which is really the best thing we can ever do for one another.

I take a seat on the porch. I am better at staying now, but I am somehow keeping one foot close to the door in case I need to bolt. I'm still holding my hand on the flusher in case I need to make a swift decision and take back the control. I am holding these precious things now, and this is the point where life turns another shade of real—when you're so in love with what you've got going on that to lose it would devastate you. You'd have to figure out how to be okay again, and you really don't want to go back and do more of that work.

_____

I think we either lean in close and risk it all, or we stay ruled by the fear of losing. In some ways, we probably lose more than we think by always holding things so tightly, so legalistically. I think God wants us to breathe, go with it, enjoy the guy who tells you not to flush him even if it isn't meant to last.

And this is what happens. The fish stays alive forever (literally, almost). Daniel and I don't. I don't understand much of why we break up so unexpectedly, but it's painful. I feel like I've been blindsided by some blunt object in the dark.

I do what I know how to do when pain hits—I get in my car, drive to Wendy's, get chicken nuggets, and call my mom while I'm crying on the couch, wrapped in a blanket, though it's ninety degrees in Atlanta.

"Hannah," she says to me through my desperate sobs, "you eat one packet of French fries. Just one. You eat them and then you go back to work. Less words, more work."

When she says this, I know my mother isn't talking about the work that happens at a desk or within the walls of a cubicle. She's talking about a work she believes we are all meant to participate in—the work of loving others despite the pain.

I don't know why I get the extreme honor of having a mother who can morph into the child of Ellen DeGeneres and Jesus at any given moment, but her words strike me. They empower me. They push me to get off the couch, after I've cried my tears, and start again.

My mother knows sympathy and the place it holds in this world. I know my mother, from eight hundred miles away, does not want to see her daughter in the throes of another failed relationship. Yet she pushes me harder and tells me to get back into the world because that's where I'm needed. Life doesn't stop because someone breaks your heart. Even with one less love story, you need to keep showing up to the life you've built.

Less words, more work. I don't control life and I don't control loss. Living fully means giving up control and still being okay with the outcome. Win or lose, you find a way to keep fighting. No matter the outcome, you keep putting your heart on the line and trying to find the best love that life can offer. The love that stays. Because honestly, what else is there?

STEAL THIS PRAYER

Dear God, don't let fear rule my story. Help me to hold things with a loose grip. I know I'm not in control. Teach me to be okay with the outcome and lead me into a life that is better than I can imagine.

| *Chapter Fifteen* | **READ THE RED TEXT** |

Faith has always been a tricky thing for me. For a long time, I didn't know what to do with it. I went to church and people told me it was important, but it was like having a juicer without an instruction manual. I knew it could do amazing things for me, help me be healthier and more holistic, but I didn't know how to turn it on.

I once heard a famous pastor from New York City say on a talk show that there's a difference between religion and relationship. He said you do one because you feel like you have to do it, and the other you do because you choose to. I really liked that. It made me think about all the times I chose a religion over a relationship and how many times, because of that legalistic structure, I ended up choosing other things over God.

I think I have a great capacity to sometimes fall into a rhythm with God that is all rules and no feelings or all feelings and no substance. I once heard a former contestant on *The Bachelor* tell a story about how she met her last boyfriend on a plane. This was years before she went on the show. It was such a serendipitous moment. For years, as they dated, she kept waiting to fully fall in love. She wanted things to click.

"I was always waiting for my feelings to catch up to the story of how we met," she said. Eventually she left because those feelings never showed up for her. All she'd been left with was a really great "how we met" story.

When I heard that story, it reminded me of God and me. Because I am that creepy person who watches *The Bachelor* and thinks about a right relationship with God. But we had a really cool "how we met" story. We met on a rainy night in a church in Chelsea, New York City. And while I still think the moment was beautiful and necessary, for a long time I waited for my feelings about faith to catch up to that heightened decision to trust God.

For years, people always asked me where God and I first met. That's a thing we talk a lot about in the church. I romanticized the story. I told it a bunch of times. I made it more dramatic than it really was. I think if we aren't careful, we stop at the "how we met" story and don't push people into better "how we are still meeting up" stories.

I'd reached the point in my faith where I didn't want my story with God to sound like a hit-and-run accident. I wanted the story to be constant and continuous. I wanted to be able to say I didn't meet him once in a church and then I talked about it for a really long time but lost all the feelings. I wanted to be able to say I met him once and that was just the beginning. Everything that happened after that first meeting? It was actually so much better and more real.

I started having all these thoughts about God and a solid relationship with him right after Daniel and I broke up. For a few weeks, Daniel and I sat in a self-constructed gray area that was really my fault. I built the gray area, if you ask me. The gray area is this in-between spot where you feel like you can't really make a decision but you know it's because you're afraid of the decision you need to make. When you're in a gray area, you don't make those concrete decisions. You kind of just sit there and hope the hard work of cutting things off for good happens all on its own.

During that "broken up but maybe not really" phase, our biggest issue was the coffee shop where he and I both liked to go. It's where we first met. It's where he asked me out on our first date. It was special to both of us, and it helped contribute to the gray area gaining more square footage.

There was this one day where I'd had a really productive writing morning. In the spirit of accomplishment, I decided to gather all my materials and head to the coffee shop. In the back of my mind, I knew Daniel would probably be there. He would see me, come over to my table, make some sly joke about how we shouldn't be talking, and then scribble something like, "You're beautiful," on a piece of notebook paper and pass it across the table to me.

I was driving to the shop and something happened. There was no music on as I turned the car right and left down side streets. That's when I heard an audible voice say inside my little Toyota Camry with the tinted drug dealer windows, "Every time you go to that coffee shop, you are choosing him over me." The voice was loud and clear. It fell down in the car like rain.

This doesn't happen often to me. I don't hear some booming voice throughout my everyday life. But I know I beg a lot to hear God, and so I have to trust that, at some points, he's speaking loud and clear to me. This was one of those points.

Ever since my depression, I'd been tiptoeing pretty carefully around God. I felt like we had grown a level deeper and there was some trust there. It's like going through a tragedy with someone else and you know you'll never be able to explain it with simple human words, so sometimes you just look at the other person and they can tell from your eyes that you remember. You don't need to say any more than that; you both know exactly where you've been and what you've come out of. That was God for me those days.

But I was being careful not to rock the boat. I wasn't really trying anything to expand my faith because I was scared if I tried, more hardship and pain would come. I didn't know if I was ready for that—until there I was, with another breakup on my hands and nowhere to look but up.

When I heard those words in the car—"you are choosing him over me"—I knew immediately that I was found out. God basically could have said anything and I would have known what he really meant: *Hey, you are avoiding me. You are tiptoeing. Why? What gives?*

I didn't go to the coffee shop that day after the God voice bellowed into the car. I turned the car around and called up my friend Gabrielle as I headed home. I asked if she'd be willing to come over. In the next few hours, Gabrielle and I fixed all the world's problems. At least that's how it feels when you've got a friend who is willing to sit beside you and just listen.

I tell her I know I am avoiding God. I tell her my reason for doing so is obvious. I'm angry and I'm upset and I'm tired of the dating game. I say I didn't sign up for heartbreak and it would have been more polite if God kindly left me out of this situation so I could move on to the next guy, the right guy.

God doesn't do that though. God uses other people, even if those other people break us open, to push us toward him.

I think he's constantly developing a bigger blueprint to drive us closer to him.

As we talk, I tell her I've never read the gospels. The gospels are the four main books in the Bible that illustrate the life of Jesus. I've read the Old Testament, I tell her, because I like the history behind it, and I've read the New Testament because I like self-help and most of the New Testament feels like self-help. Somehow those words "I've never read them" just slip out.

"Why do you think you've never read the gospels?" she asks me.

"I don't know," I answer. "I guess I'm just afraid."

"Afraid of what?"

"I'm afraid because people talk so much about how Jesus changes everything. And what if it isn't actually true? What if I read the gospels and nothing changes?"

Since stepping through the back door of faith, I've been on board with most parts of spirituality. I like reading the Bible. I go to church. I enjoy the music. I am even cool with God and letting him change me. But for reasons I still cannot fully explain, I never want to talk about Jesus.

People talk a lot about Jesus in the South. Even more astonishing, when you go through a breakup, a crazy number of people tell you that you just need to date Jesus. Just date Jesus, and your heart will be put back together.

I don't know how you (1) date someone you can't touch, (2) date someone who has a Holy Spirit sidekick/counterpart, and (3) ever get over the fact that your boyfriend took away the sins of the world. You're never going to be the impressive one in that relationship. You'll always be dating up. Out of your league. Maybe that's the point?

People say things like "you just need to date Jesus" or "you're too far from him." They make it seem like they are holding a map up to your face and can chart exactly where you are on it. They make it seem like they know—because they're experts at longitude and latitude—that you are not close enough to God at that moment.

There are a lot of words that get said to single people that I wish I could blot out on behalf of God, because God never wants a person to feel like they are incomplete or "not there yet." So I will veer off course for a second and speak loud and clear to the single people out there: I'm sorry. I'm sorry on behalf of anyone who ever told you your heart wasn't close enough to God for love. God isn't looking at you and seeing some half-complete, could-do-better version. He looks at you and sees love. I know it's hard to believe that, but the most valuable thing I've ever learned as a single person is to release this fear that I wouldn't meet someone until I was perfectly content with God. That always made me feel like I was wrong or like I wasn't "there" yet. Now I just believe God has good timing.

In the meantime, you are allowed. You are allowed to fall apart when you get your heart broken. You are allowed to hurt just because you don't want to be alone anymore. You are allowed to be mad. You are allowed to release that pain whenever you want to release that pain. This isn't about you and whatever it is that other people tell you needs to be done; you need to decide you are ready on your own. When you are ready to fly, you will. And if you're scared of that flight, try anyway.

I don't let the idea of dating Jesus go in the next few days. I decided that if people are flippantly going to tell me to date my Messiah, then I will do it. I will do it to prove a point, and I will be the best dang girlfriend to Jesus that the world had ever seen. If Jesus wants me as his girlfriend, then he needs to be prepared to get sick of me fast, because I am about to be the ultimate, stage-5 clinger girlfriend. I am about to be sitting outside his house, texting him for his whereabouts. I am about to be stealing his phone and checking his messages. This is how close I plan to get.

Gabrielle and I come up with a plan for dating Jesus. We plot out that I'll go to a different coffee shop across Atlanta every morning before work for the "date." I will commit to being up earlier in the morning so that each "date" can go anywhere from an hour to two hours. This is normally the window of time I'd be willing to give a perfect stranger who matched with me on a dating application, so I thought that I should be willing to give this same amount of time to God.

The goal is to visit a new coffee shop each day, especially since I'm now exiled from the one coffee shop that made Atlanta home for me. If you know anything about Atlanta, there is no lack of coffee shops. A new coffee shop is born every five minutes. A new coffee shop is spreading its wings and beginning to fly as you read this today.

I will start at Chrome Yellow, snake my way toward Condesa Coffee, spend some time at the Chattahoochee Coffee Company, hang out at Revelator, revisit the three Octanes, and hit up Dancing Goats.

"Something will change," Gabrielle says to me. "I promise you, something will change."

"How do I start then?"

"You show up at the coffee shop. You open the Bible. You start with one gospel. Pick John—it's the most descriptive of all of them. Read John as many times as you can throughout the next week. That's your goal: Read only John as many times as you can read it in the next week. Don't stop to pull the words apart or study them closer. Just read."

"And then spend a week reading Matthew, a week reading Luke, and a week reading Mark."

"Just reading it?"

"Yes, reading it as much as you can, as many times as you can. Just take simple notes. Answer one question as you go: Who does God show himself to be in this?"

"Okay," I say. "I can do this."

"You can absolutely do this," she says. "We will all be here when you get back."

I sometimes think a lot of people meet God twice. There's the initial meeting and then there's another one, somewhere down the line, when you meet him again, but he's different. You need him for a different reason. The stakes are higher. The questions are bigger. I know I met God twice. And the second time, I learned something new—all for myself this time.

The morning after talking with Gabrielle, I wake up to go meet Jesus. I feel like a sixth grader on their first day of middle school, nervous to know what it's going to be like. I put my Bible and notebook into a bag and clutch the straps of my backpack as I walk toward the first coffee shop and find a seat in the corner. I remind myself there is nothing to be afraid of. Really, this is all just an experiment, and it will either work brilliantly or not at all. I am open to both at this point.

I begin with the book of John. It's a weird place to begin getting to know your boyfriend for the first time. You learn, right out the gate, that your guy is the light of the world. Before the first chapter even ends, your boyfriend is busy calling out disciples to follow him, and in the second chapter, he's supplying wine at a wedding that clearly didn't plan well for their rowdy guests. Your boyfriend is super hospitable. The more you get to know this guy Jesus, the more you realize you're pretty small in comparison. The two of you are an unlikely couple. He's way too good for you. To top it all off, he's a carpenter, which means he's rugged and can build furniture (two of the most underrated attributes in the world).

But I do exactly what Gabrielle tells me to do—I keep notes on who God is in each of the stories. For as long as I've been studying the Bible, never once have I asked myself that question: *Who is God in this story?* My knee-jerk reaction is always to pick through the story until I can find myself in it. I am the rich young ruler. I am the woman by the well. I am Judas. I am Simon Peter. I am Martha. I am the good Samaritan. I am the tax collector. The Bible should be renamed at this point, "Me. All day. Every day. Me."

No one ever taught me how to look for anyone other than myself in the Bible stories. The sermons I listened to were always about me; the songs I sang were always about me. I knew that Jesus loved me, but that idea of love only ran a few inches deep, because no one had never told me to stop and figure out how he loved me. No one ever told me I could dig a few feet deeper and find something other than myself to fill me up.

Jesus and I cruise all over Atlanta together, pulling into coffee shops like old friends. We sip lattes together. We try to drink our coffee black, like the real diehard coffee drinkers. We grow a level deeper, and my heartbreak begins to lift.

Brooke, my Texas Proud friend, decides to join me. She tells me she is willing to dig wherever I am digging in the gospels. When we meet up, I'm in Luke, and so she pulls out her Bible and flips to Luke.

Her Bible is covered in notes. You can barely read the lines of the text from all the things she has written in the margins.

"Luke is one of my favorites," she says as she is flipping there. "Good ole Luke."

Turns out, Brooke doesn't want to wait any longer. She means it when she says she wants to start digging. Right now. Today.

"Oh, this is one of my favorite stories," she says to me, pointing to Luke 1. "John the Baptist is born to Elizabeth and Zechariah. Elizabeth is barren and old. God promised her a baby, but it just doesn't seem possible."

Brooke goes on to tell me that an angel comes to them and promises them a son. His name will be John. The angel is right—God is faithful. But the story doesn't end there.

"I mean, God could have just been faithful and given them a son, an ordinary son," Brooke says. "But he gives them *the* John the Baptist, who leads the way for Jesus! God didn't let them play some ordinary role. He gave them much better than ordinary."

As Brooke and I begin studying every Tuesday and Thursday of that month, I learn that Brooke lives in this "better" state of mind. Her faith isn't average and her hope in God isn't small. She is constantly believing that God is doing something far from ordinary. Our meetings start at 6:30 in the morning, and we sometimes stay there for three hours at a time. The text transforms in front of my eyes. I stop reading it like it's bland, and Brooke shows me how to add salt and other spices. Brooke shows me this isn't just words we're consuming; this is meat. This is filling. This is something happening here and now; it's not some expired story from thousands of years ago.

As I read that month, I kept thinking back to one of the most beautiful depictions of the gospel ever given to me by my friend Caroline. It was a few years ago, before I lived in Georgia. She and I were sitting at a high-top table in a dive bar in Connecticut listening to obscure, unheard-of bands play. She was there to cheer on a friend, so she invited me to come along.

Caroline is no-nonsense. She's an engineer, and I found a deeper level of faith when I met her because I thought to myself, *This girl has no time for stuff that is silly or not real.* I think sometimes people make faith seem so elementary and almost ridiculous that you wonder why you're giving so much of your life to it. Then you meet someone like Caroline, who doesn't mess around and really doesn't have time to mess around, and she believes so adamantly that it makes you want to believe even more.

So Caroline was sitting there, wearing a sweatshirt with Minnie Mouse on the front, and nearly out of nowhere she just blurted out, "If the gospel is what we say it is, then it can be summed up in three words: It is finished. That's it. That's all. Show is over. No more shame. No more doubt. No more guilt. If I believe that the gospel is really Jesus finishing it all for us, then I am just called to dance in the aftermath of what he did."

I think Caroline was right. The gospel is this astonishing story line where we were once people who had cause to be filled with fear, doubt, anxiety, and death. We were swimming in it, and it was brutal. And then this man comes along and his name is Jesus. He walks differently; he doesn't have those chains we put on ourselves. And then, in unforgettable fashion, he dies for us. He dies for the things we did wrong in the past and what we will surely mess up in the future. And what's really supposed to happen when you put your trust in Jesus is you're supposed to live in the context of a different story. You're supposed to move out of the apartment where Fear and Doubt are your anxious landlords, and you are supposed to figure out how to live in this new place where Joy and Peace are your roommates.

We are supposed to let the fear and the doubt and the shame go. We are supposed to walk in a new way. We are supposed to be so thankful for this gift God gave us, this exchange, that all we can really do to express our gratitude is choose to dance in the aftermath of what Jesus did for us. I say "supposed to" because I think some of us could do a much better job focusing on that story line. I know a lot of people who believe in the story of Jesus but have more fear than people who don't believe in anything at all. I want something different. I want a reason to dance.

It makes me think of the story I heard about how the movie *Frozen* came to be. In the original script, Elsa—the main character—was meant to be a villain. They say her character originally looked edgy, like Amy Winehouse. Two songwriters for the film—Kristen Anderson-Lopez and Robert Lopez—were spinning their wheels day after day, coming up with songs that kept ending up on the editing room floor. They were trying to create a catchy villain song, but the tune that stuck, the tune that surprised everyone in the room when they heard it for the first time, was the song "Let It Go"—the powerful ballad about letting go of fear and walking into a new life.

Codirector of the film Jennifer Lee said in the *New York Times*, "The minute we heard the song the first time, I knew that I had to rewrite the whole movie."[1] A song that was only meant to be a side thought on the soundtrack ended up informing and rescripting the whole plot so Elsa could become this troubled character who was redeemed by the love of her sister.

I'm willing to bet that none of the people sitting in the boardroom on the day the song "Let It Go" was played for the first time went home that night and listened to all the reject songs. There wasn't a need to go back to the songs that weren't as good. They had the hit. They had the story that changed the entire story.

I think the gospels are the song that rewrites the whole story. If we believe the story of Jesus in those four books, if we take it for what it is and believe it's the best story out there for us, then it's meant to rewrite our whole entire story from start to finish. It's meant to change us as characters, remake us into characters who are no longer crippled by fear and doubt but dancing in the aftermath of a bigger story.

I want to rest inside this. I want to know it's true every single day of my life. I'd be lying if I didn't say there are still days when I doubt or give fear too much breath. But there's a simple prayer for that, one prayed by the father of a suffering boy, that I borrow often: God, "I do believe; help me overcome my unbelief!" (Mark 9:24).

If I could add on to the father's prayer in that moment, if he would just pass me the prayer microphone, I would say, "Help

---

1. Melena Ryzik, "The Nominees Are Blockbusters: Oscar-Nominated Songs with Familiar Composers," *New York Times*, February 19, 2014, www.nytimes .com/2014/02/20/movies/awardsseason/oscar-nominated-songs-with-familiar -composers.html.

me to believe there is a better story out there than the one I try to live out on my own. I don't want a story where fear is the focal point, the main character with the most lines. I want a story about love. I want a story where love saves and redeems and makes me whole. Help me invest in this story and believe it with all I've got so I can feel freedom, so I can feel like the story changes me and I'm better because of it."

This isn't a selfish prayer. It's a real prayer. In his 1,027th sermon (because someone counted for the man), Charles Spurgeon said, "Never be content with hearing a sermon unless you can understand it, and if there is a truth that is above you, strain after it, strive to know it."[2] I think the worst thing we could possibly do is accept something just because someone told us to or because everyone else in the room is nodding their heads. We have to feel it in our bones. It must change us. We need to know it as our truth, and I think that only comes from digging deeper and asking all our questions.

STEAL THIS PRAYER

Dear God, meet me. There are times when I cannot feel you, when all I can pray is, "God, help me with this unbelief." As I sit with my Bible, amplify the pages and the stories within them. Reveal yourself to me in crazy ways when I walk outside today. Take these small hours I can offer you and help me climb to new levels in my faith.

---

2. Charles Spurgeon, "The Joy of the Lord, the Strength of His People," December 31, 1871, Sermon No. 1027, https://answersingenesis.org/education/spurgeon-sermons/1027-the-joy-of-the-lord-the-strength-of-his-people.

| Chapter Sixteen | # ASK ALL YOUR QUESTIONS |

The best lesson I ever learned about faith came from a seventy-seven-year-old atheist named Joe, whom I met at a Starbucks one morning right before I moved to Atlanta, before any of this story really even existed.

He approached my table while I was working one morning, stretched out his hand, and said, "Joe."

I pulled the headphones from my ears.

"Hannah," I answered back, taking his hand.

"Hannah," he repeated the name back to me. "What is it that you love?"

"What is it that I love?" I had to repeat the question to make sure I heard him right. It's sad that we don't really ask that question often. We ask questions like, "What do you do?" and we assign worth to a person based on their answer.

I start telling Joe that I love words. I love nouns and verbs.

"If there had been a way to take a semicolon to the senior prom, I would have done it."

He smiled at me kindly and pulled up a seat to sit down.

"What do *you* love?" I asked him.

"Math," he answered, nearly instantly. "I love math."

"My worst subject in school," I said. "They had to create a

whole new class in high school for me because I couldn't pass algebra. I'm just not good at it."

Joe reached across the table before I could finish explaining. He took my notebook and picked up the pen next to my laptop. Opening to a clean page, Joe began scribbling something down on the paper. He turned the paper over and pushed it back toward me.

"What is the answer to that problem?"

The math problem on the piece of paper involved fractions. I knew immediately that I didn't know the answer.

"I don't know," I said.

"That!" he exclaimed as he stood and lifted his finger to the ceiling. "That is the reason why I love math!"

I stared at him as he went on. "If I asked you what's the capital of Arizona and you couldn't Google it or phone a friend, you'd have to tell me, 'I don't know,' but I've given you everything you need to solve this problem, and so the answer is never 'I don't know'; it's simply, 'I don't know yet.'"

I don't know yet. There is something so powerful about those four words sitting beside one another. It fills you with this sort of belief that you aren't as lost as you think you are. You've got everything you need to solve the problem. Just start asking yourself the right questions.

So if you came to me, sat across the table from me, and asked, "Where do I start? Where do I go to meet God for a first or second time?" I'd tell you to sit with the Bible. Lay your "I don't know yet" on the table and just keep it there.

I would tell you to just start at the beginning. That's what I did. Making time to meet with him every day became a priority. I began looking forward to it. I could see a difference in the days when I spent the first hour with God and the days when I chose something else. I found myself holding a lot more questions than answers and realizing I had nowhere to drop them but in that quiet, uninterrupted meeting with God.

Read the story for ten minutes or twenty. Get honest. Maybe say a simple prayer like, "God, show me who you are in all of this." Just try to find God in the story. I think you can approach God with the mind-set of a journalist—God would rather you dig for the details than take his sound bites and run. Write down every question you have. It takes time. Give yourself the grace to be in the process as you're figuring it out.

Comically, last year I failed to follow this very advice I'm giving you right now. I decided I wanted to read the Bible in one year. It was a part of my New Year's resolutions and overall plans to be a better human. For anyone who has ever tried to read the Bible in a year, you already know it's a lot of Bible. A lot of "every day." I went strong for the first few days and then started missing days. I missed one day and then another. I missed a whole week. Suddenly I was behind the pack and they were all ahead of me, and I felt left out and defeated.

I was sitting with a friend one night, hashing out my Bible FOMO feelings with him, and he asked me why I had such an enormous need to catch up. Like, why scramble to read through all the missed pages quickly just to stay with the group? Wouldn't I miss the marrow? Wouldn't I miss the purpose?

I hadn't even thought about it that way. My goal was to read the Bible to grow closer to God. But the way I was acting was translating into, "I'm reading so that I can prove to others that I was capable of doing this challenge." That's the danger of goal setting—we set noteworthy goals more for other people than for ourselves.

Truthfully, I rarely think about God when I set most goals for myself. Even worse, I set a lot of "God goals" but still act like he isn't in them.

"Just start where you are," my friend told me.

Just start where you are. I tell myself this will be the hum of my new year. This will be my challenge: to go to God and start in prayer by saying, "Here I am, Lord. Here I am with my palms up and my heart ready for you to do the work in me. This is honesty hour. I've got a lot of doubts, a lot of stuff to work out, but I'm asking you to start with me here in this humbled, low-to-the-ground space. Just start with me here."

So I started over again with new zeal. This time, I waited for all the people to begin their race. I watched them sprint out of the gates with Bibles in their hands. And then, when I felt like it, I begin. I didn't pick a reading plan. I didn't set up a schedule. I just opened up to the first page of Genesis and started to read. I wrote in the margins everything I could learn about God from reading the text.

I found myself looking forward to reading more than anything else in my day once I got going. I carried my Bible through the airport with me. It didn't feel like I was reading a rulebook this time, or only reading to check a chunk of Scripture off a list. This time I read the book as if it were a novel, a great story that you don't stop to analyze along the way.

Turns out, the Bible is all about process. It's this beautiful book of stories and poems and prose about being human and needing something bigger to take over the story line. It's story after story about how we think we are really cool and strong and independent. People are constantly choosing themselves over God. It gets a little bit draining and a little bit sad. The Old Testament makes you feel like you're carrying around some extra weight because you suddenly get it—you get why the character of Jesus is necessary to stop the madness.

I got stuck on the character of Moses as I read. I am willing to bet Moses had a lot of "I don't know yet" moments with God. I actually fell in love with Moses as I started talking about him as if he were still alive. I thought about being Moses's girl-friend and giving him back massages after long days with the cranky Israelites. I imagined that Moses looked exactly like Milo Ventimiglia, the dad on *This Is Us*. It took me weeks to get over the fact that God told Moses he couldn't go to the Promised Land. I didn't think it was fair, but I didn't want to argue with God either.

I cried ugly, uncivilized tears all throughout Deuteronomy. Deuteronomy is like Moses's farewell tour. It's his final words. It's like your favorite author writing one last book before they die. This is how I saw Deuteronomy after I'd spent so much time with Moses.

I cried even harder because Moses knew humanity. He knew the people who had been following him to the Promised Land all this time, and he knew, without a doubt, that they were going to mess up and stray from God. They would pick other things. They would try to fill their holes in other ways. He wouldn't be able to stop them. He wouldn't be able to control them. And it broke his heart.

I pictured Moses with his rugged beard, standing before the

crowd of people and telling them, "Be strong. Be brave. Don't let the fear get in the way, because your God is going ahead of you. He's got this. He won't let you down; he won't leave you." And then he went off and died. I watched Moses go away forever on February 22, 2017, at 10:42 a.m. I know this because I sent an email to a friend with the subject line "Moses died today."

I think it's really beautiful that, from the beginning of time, the message about God has never changed: He is here. He is with us. He is always inviting us into the story.

A friend of mine says we can ask God all of our questions. He isn't going to hush us or act like he's never heard that one before. We are allowed to have every sort of emotion before God, and that's what makes it all so real.

As I read, I realize there are questions. There are big questions. I need entire therapy sessions devoted to the books of Joshua and Judges. There are things that happen in the Bible I can't wrap my brain around. I'd call my mom after I finished reading a big chunk of Scripture and we'd talk about the things we didn't understand or the things she didn't catch the first time around.

There's a story in the Bible about a guy named Jephthah, who gets in trouble and offers up his daughter as a sacrifice. The poor girl doesn't even have a chance to get married. She asks her father if, before she dies, she could go away with her girlfriends for a weekend to mourn her forever singleness. It's the strangest story. I don't understand it. I'm actually quite disturbed by it. I come to find there are more and more of these stories every time I go back to the text. But what these stories do is start a conversation. They fuel more questions. Faith becomes something I don't follow blindly; it becomes something I wrestle with and make my own.

No one ever told me I would need to wrestle with my faith. My faith was handed to me prepackaged, and I'm learning, as I sit with God, that I am not meant to blindly accept that. I am meant to pull out all the ingredients and prepare it. I am meant to make it my own. I need to fight to believe in something bigger than me, to give that thing new weight and meaning all the time.

I know I'll never get to the end of my life and say, "God, here is my faith. It was contained in pews and hymns." I am going to say that the inventory of my faith was a lot of uncertainty, a good mother, the feeling of grace, a yellow room, a man who loved me through the throes of doubts, the play *Les Misérables*, a slew of coffee shops, and Bible stories I didn't quite understand.

I want my faith inventory to be that personal and intimate. Theologian Henri Nouwen says there's no happy medium to intimacy. He says intimacy is beyond fear, and I love that idea.[1] I love imagining we can step into this meeting space with God and the fear just knows it can't come in. I think about how Moses is named in the Bible as the one who experienced intimacy with God. And yet Moses questions everything. He constantly asks God for signs, being insecure about himself. Eventually, God gets exasperated with Moses, but he never gives up on him. I think to myself, *I want Moses's faith. I want to be bold enough to ask God all my questions.*

I feel the most loved when people ask me deep questions. It makes me feel like they've thought a lot about me. It makes me

---

1. Henri Nouwen, *Lifesigns: Intimacy, Fecundity, and Ecstasy in Christian Perspective* (New York: Crown, 2013), 24.

feel as though they've been paying attention. In a world where it's hard to keep someone's attention for more than five minutes before they start reaching in their bag to grab the phone, having someone's attention is one of the best feelings in the world. It makes you feel alive. Grounded. Fully present and fully here.

I think God gave me this attribute. And since I believe I'm made in the likeness of God, I believe God must love it too when we ask our questions, when we stand before him and say, "Show me things. Help me make this faith my own. Help me hear you, I know you're talking back."

Grace and mercy are found in asking big questions. To ask big questions is to go before a God who can handle all parts of us—our junk, our nastiness, our hopes, our failures. I think God is big enough for our big questions and bigger frustrations.

The answers may not come dramatically. They may not be right in front of my face. But maybe if I keep going, keep asking all the questions that are laid on my heart, something miraculous might happen. I might find a few answers, or I might find peace in the not knowing.

My favorite element of God is the not knowing. I love that about my relationship with God. I love that there are gray areas. I love that I cannot possibly be wise enough to understand all that this life has given me. There are dozens of things reported in the news or taking place in my personal life that leave me raising my hands, shrugging my shoulders, and saying, "I'm not really sure. I don't get it." It's not always mine to get.

Learning the elements of God is like learning the traits of someone you start falling in love with. If you spend enough time with them, you begin to see things that weren't there before. You think to yourself, *I didn't know this about you. This is another element of you. A sweet detail. I love trying to understand you. Maybe I could make a lifetime out of getting to know you better.*

I feel that way about God. I think my heart would be broken in two if the day ever came when the learning stopped and I suddenly knew everything there was to know. That's the beauty of God: you can spend your whole life "coming to know him" and still never touch the tip of what he is.

So here's a prayer. It's simple. It's not wordy. You can say it under your breath in a coffee shop and no one will look at you strange. It's a prayer I prayed, and it turned my world upside down: *If you are real, God, then be real. Be real in my life.*

STEAL THIS PRAYER

Dear God, be real in my life. There is a layer of intimacy I cannot get to when I'm always concerned with "right" and "wrong." Help me to be brave enough to ask the questions and sit in the unknown. Come and join me in the unknown and reveal things to me there I've never seen before.

Chapter Seventeen	# STARVE THE LIONS

When you're an artist living in a big city and wanting to marry an accountant, you've really got no choice but to use a dating application. You can't ask your other artist friends to set up a meet-cute with you and all of their finance friends. They are likely to shrug their shoulders and tell you they have nothing of the sort. It's a real bummer you can only file your taxes once instead of speed-dating your way through a slew of accountants as they help you write stuff off. I don't even know when I picked up the accountant dream, but I think I fell in love with the stability that seems to present itself in accounting for numbers. It seemed like the complete opposite of me, and you know what they say: opposites attract.

At this point in my life—twenty-seven and "perpetually single," as I've dubbed myself—my friends think I should drop the accountant dream. Even my therapist tells me I need to let it go. I don't understand why though. I don't have some long list of must-have attributes. I'm not specifying hair color or requesting certain interests for the guy. I have two hopes about the guy I will marry: must love numbers and must wear black socks.

It was probably the worst idea in the world to move to Georgia, specifically the South, at the age of twenty-five while still single. Marriage is a thing here. Getting married young feels

193

like an unspoken expectation. I'm seeing values change a little bit as I live here longer, but I don't enjoy my time spent in the Single Girls of America club. I find the meetings to not be fun. I find there aren't good snacks. Everyone seems to have a dismal demeanor, like the apocalypse may fall on our heads before a decent man takes us out to dinner. I want a different attitude about dating and eventual marriage.

I used to think another person could complete me. Now I know the opposite. A person can only add on to you. They will show you reality. They will push you out of your comfort zone. They may buy you roses and tell you that you look good in blue, but they will never complete you. Another person will never step outside today and live for you. There's no ribbon-cutting ceremony the second you meet someone where the mayor hands you secret keys to the city and says, "Congratulations, you are complete now. You're never going to have to wonder who you are again." If anything, I think falling in love makes you question "who you are" in the sight of God more frequently. You and I are forever a process. Thank God, we are forever a process.

Throughout that month when I tried to date Jesus, I actually figured out how to take myself on dates. That was ground-breaking for me. Don't worry, it didn't get weird. I didn't sit at tables by myself and compliment myself or try to hold my own hand. I just decided to silence the lie in my brain that tried to tell me I couldn't go and do "that" until I met someone. I stopped waiting to live. I went out and got dinner for one. I had intimate nights where it was just me and a cookbook and a batch of eggplant, trying to make vegetarian lasagna work. I took myself to Graceland in Memphis, bought a ticket for one, and happily strolled through the home of Elvis while the voice of John Stamos told me about the carpet and furniture in each room.

Something really beautiful happened when I stopped waiting for someone to show up. I stopped being so fearful about being single. I stopped viewing it as an accident or God's blind spot. And as I took the time to just create my own adventures, I figured out who I was. I didn't hitch my worth to anyone else. I didn't check my phone incessantly, hoping to get a text. I just woke up and made decisions for myself. I figured out what I bring to the table and what I'm good at. When you know that, it's even easier to date someone else. You know your strengths and you know what you are looking for in another human being. This time, it's not because you need to be completed; it's because you want a complement. When I stopped needing to be sure of the person on the other side of the dating application, I became sure of myself.

A month after breaking up with Daniel, I download a dating app. My expectations couldn't get lower to the ground. *It can only get better from here*, I think. I pick up my "accountant with black socks" category once again and keep marching forward. The name of the application is called Hinge. My friend from New York City recommended it to me.

"I've been on a couple of good dates," she said. "They have jobs. Real jobs."

Now I'm here, with another pile of men's faces staring back at me from the screen, and I think to myself, *Here we are again. Same rules: Show up but don't reach out. Wait for them to say hi first.* I am trying to adapt eighteenth-century chivalry to online dating. I stay on my eighteenth-century high horse until I get matched with a guy named Lane. I get off the horse. I salivate. I plot a pickup line because I'm usually pretty good with those.

When you get matched with someone on the application, the app sends you a message that's pretty corny, like, "You're a match made in heaven! It's time to start chatting! Here are a few ways to break the ice!" And then they give you some questions you can ask the other person:

- What is your biography in five emojis?
- Do you like pumpkin spice? (it's October)

So I decide to give Lane the option. I type out a message: "There are some pretty tempting icebreakers to use on you . . ."

Five hours later, I get a message. It's two words: "Try me."

"It's either a yay or nay to pumpkin spice lattes or tell me your biography in five emojis. Welcome to 2015!"

I think I am being cool. He doesn't respond.

I should say that this is all happening the weekend of my big brother's wedding. I flew home to Connecticut to be a bridesmaid in the wedding. I first send the message to Lane before the rehearsal dinner. I feel beautiful that night and confident because I truly think I'm going to like this guy. By eight o'clock the next morning I'm a wreck because I realize I am the idiot who asked a grown man for his biography in five emojis.

We spend the whole day in a hotel room getting ready. Hair happens and then makeup. We take pictures. We rehearse. We take more pictures. I am checking my phone between things. I don't mean to seem neurotic, but at this point, I'm just terribly embarrassed. I debated deleting the application entirely.

We line up. We process down the aisle. I stand in the row beside my soon-to-be sister-in-law's sisters. There are three of them and then me. My brother's bride begins coming down the stairs, arm linked with her father's. And suddenly, my brother is weeping. He is weeping violently. He is red in the face and cannot control himself. I've seen my brother cry approximately once in my life before. Other than that, I wondered if maybe he was emotionless. He is crying so hard he can barely make out the vows he wrote for her.

Everyone in the room is crying. I am crying as I clutch my bouquet, and I say under my breath, "God, I know you haven't forgotten about me. I believe you haven't forgotten about me." I want this thing, this thing called "love," so badly. Sometimes you just want to know someone is coming for you too.

We go into the reception. I feel awkward the whole time as guests ask me how I am liking Atlanta, if I've met anyone. I'm surrounded by girls I went to high school with who ended up in serious relationships with guys my brother's age. I feel out of place. I keep ducking into the bathroom to check my phone. No answers.

Around 10 p.m., I leave the wedding. They will be partying all night and I have a 7 a.m. flight back to Atlanta. Ten thirty rolls around and I get a message back from Lane. No "hi." No "how are you." Just five emojis, all in a row. One is of an angel. Another is of a little boy running.

In my desperate attempt to just talk to this man more, I tell Lane I am a world-class emoji interpreter and that I'm going to share with him a little bit about his life. I make up some elaborate story based on his five emojis, and then I shove five of my own emojis back at him and tell him he needs to interpret them. I will make conversation with this man, even if it kills me.

I don't remember which emojis I sent to him, but he responded back with a story: A fierce girl ventured out in the vast ocean, dished out plenty of gifts, felt like a foreign girl until she realized she was an angel.

A week and a half later, after spending every night talking and me realizing he was, indeed, an accountant, we went on our first date. "Honesty Hour" might be an intimidating exercise for a first date, yet that's exactly what Lane and I did. I don't know how it happened, but I know I brought it up first. I was sick of playing games. I was sick of all the light "get-to-know-you banter" that happens on a first date. I wanted to get right to the point and figure it out: Are we in this or not?

I know we broke every first date rule as we talked about past relationships and shortcomings in our own lives. I found myself saying out loud to him, "This is an honesty hour."

"Honesty hour?" he asked.

"Yes, honesty hour. In honesty hour you get to say whatever you want."

"Okay," he answered with a nod. "Honesty hour. Let's go."

And so, for the rest of that date, we stayed within honesty hour, and it was refreshing and like breath to the parts of me that always feel the need to be polished and insightful. When we said risky things, we could preface it with, "After all, this is honesty hour." And there was no judgment or worry sitting between us. It felt really good. It felt really safe. It felt like we were handing one another permission slips—permission to be in process.

I want my whole life to be just as real as the conversation that night beneath the twinkle lights. The two of us talking so furiously that eventually the wait staff stopped checking in and left us to our outside table and the hints of an Atlanta summer still competing with the October air. I want my life to be one big honesty hour between me, God, the people who've found something, the people who've lost something, and all who sit in between. I want it to be ever-expanding and ever-inviting. I want a faith that says, *There's always more room at the table. Come be in process with us.*

———————

I knew really early on that Lane was my person. I wasn't expecting it to happen that fast, but little things made it clear, like the day I came home to a vase of flowers sitting on the front step with a note inside that read, "A fierce girl ventured out in the vast ocean, dished out plenty of gifts, felt like a foreign girl until she realized she was an angel."

On our third date, he cooked me scallops at his home. He showed up at the door to let me in with an easy smile and a flannel. He bought me a bottle of wine with a gold-glinted wrapping because he said the story on the back of the bottle was something I would like. It was all about roots and finding your home. We baked brownies and watched *Garden State.* It was the first time I knew I could build a life with this man. I think realizing you can build a life with someone is a different feeling than the one you get when they take you on extravagant dates. I'd gone on the dates with all the impressive stunts pulled out. This was something slower, something surer.

Even with this deep knowing in my gut that I'd found a man to cover my thin places, I had all this anxiety about fourth and fifth dates. I'd scripted this untrue story in my brain before I met him that I was never going to be certain when the right one was standing in front of me. I would never have a way of knowing. That story was dangerous, because the more I told it to myself, the harder it became to undo it. The story gained power. The story had momentum.

Anxiety will have a field day with whatever you feed it. Your anxiety is happy to feed on your love life, your relationships, your career, and your purpose in life. Your anxiety wants to be fed something substantial, something that matters most to you, so it can feel full and still hold a purpose in your brain.

At one point, I try to distance myself from Lane. I figure eventually we'll break up anyway so I should probably leave first. I pull back from texting him. I didn't want to hurt him. I text him one evening to ask him what he's doing. I'm sitting in my car and it's dark outside. I've just gotten home from a meeting, and he tells me he just finished reading Ezra. I don't know a ton about Ezra. In fact, I know little to nothing about that Bible book, so I'm impressed. If Lane is trying to impress me in this moment, it's working. I admire any man who sits and reads Ezra as a hobby on a Tuesday night.

When I get inside my house, I pull a Bible from the shelf and flip the pages to Ezra. Here's what's crazy about that: At the beginning of Ezra, something happens. The king in the land at the time decides to free all the captives in Babylon who've been enduring their exile. It's the conclusion to Jeremiah's prophecy about the people living in exile for seventy years, building houses, making babies, and praying a lot. It's the promise now coming to fruition.

In all that time I spent reading about the people in exile, I never once imagined their freedom. I never knew that part of the story. I had those people living in Babylon forever in my brain. I never bothered to read more to see how the story ended.

In that moment, I felt God. I felt him all over my relationship with Lane. I think fear helps us live in self-preservation mode sometimes. I think that is fear's biggest hope—that we'll play it safe. But if we feed the fear too much, we start to live in a self-made prison. We build our own exile. We give ourselves our own seventy-year sentence. We forget about hope. We forget about love.

I had to make the decision at that point in the relationship to not feed Lane to the lions of anxiety in my head. I told Lane about my anxiety, how real it was. I told Lane the anxiety I was experiencing made me want to run, but he had to know that it wasn't because of him. I told the anxiety, *After tonight, this is not your home. You don't get to live inside this relationship anymore.*

I really said those things. I really kicked the anxiety out of the relationship and spent hours in the next few weeks continuing to kick it out. Every time it came back, looking for a home, I turned it away. I wanted Lane's love for me to finally have the chance to be bigger than the fears that I let half-love me my whole life.

You are allowed to starve your anxiety and leave it homeless. It's hard work. It's constant work. It wasn't instant. There were no fireworks or planes whizzing by spelling out his name. Like everything else I'd experienced in the last year, I finally understood that love, too, would be a process of peeling off the layers and letting yourself be fully seen by someone else.

———

They say love is made by the attraction of opposites. Yes and no. Lane loves numbers, and I swoon over words. He likes old-time country music, and I prefer rappers with a life expectancy of thirty years. But I don't think love works if two people have an opposite expectation of what respect looks like or how communication unfolds. Love withers if and when we seek opposition in faith or loyalty or truth. That doesn't mean you can't ask questions or disagree on things. It's the "seeking opposition" that will become a bigger mess.

Love isn't a feeling. It's not listening to your heart and chasing whatever desire emerges from that organ. My heart wants different things every day of the week. There's a steadier drumbeat inside me that wants to pick the things I know are good for me, lovely, constant, steadfast. It's training myself to listen for that beat.

Love is like purchasing an old car that used to drive like a dream. It's slowly but steadily replacing the engine, putting in new brakes, lifting up the hood and seeing what's making the thing sputter and stall. It's an understanding that the greatest treasures in this world demand time and energy, endless tune-ups, and chances to ask, "What's wrong now?" You think to yourself, *The rest of the world might not always see it, but I love this little car. I love that it's mine.*

Love is a holy and cool sanctification process that keeps me in awe of God and needing God more every time Lane says my name. It's making a decision one night to drown out your fear and say, "Wow. Hmm. Crazy. At last? You're here? Let's go." So now we're marching, hand in hand, thinking of an eternity after this life that drives like a dream.

I don't think "the one" is a feeling that tramples over you

like a pit bull. "The one" is just a person, like you. They will be imperfect and salty. They will let you down and forget important dates. They will burn the toast and sing out of tune sometimes. "The one" is just a person in your life who gets your extra portions of grace.

"The one" is just a person who gets the majority of your texts, tears, and prayers. They pick you. You pick them. It's like picking your kickball team every morning when you wake up: you pick them, even when they have a bum ankle.

Love is not a club; it's a choice. Love is not running for the presidency just because you have a need to win. Love isn't getting every vote. Love is being a candidate. It is a long stretch of victories and defeats. You keep running hard. You keep running fast. And one day you crash into someone who really sees you, who sees your issues like you always hoped your issues would be seen—as their own.

STEAL THIS PRAYER

Dear God, take away my fear and morph it into love. Remind me not to feed the lions in my brain. I so badly want to use my best energy to be thankful instead of fearful. Cover my days in real and lasting love. Teach me an anthem of love over fear.

Chapter Eighteen | GET OUT OF THE WAY

My friend Jerome says there are only two kinds of emotions: love and fear. Everything else stems from those two. You either operate in love, or you operate in fear.

Last month, I went to a conference in San Antonio, Texas. My trips to speak somewhere usually last twenty-four hours, but I spent four days in Texas, speaking on different days and writing when I didn't need to be at the conference.

The way I start writing is usually the same every time. I find a quiet space. I place my computer beside me. I open my Bible, and I either return to a space in the text where I've been digging, or I ask God to send me somewhere new.

This doesn't always work. I've definitely had my fair share of times when I felt led to a part of the Bible that doesn't actually exist. But on this day, I put my head on the floor of the hotel room in San Antonio. I fold my knees underneath me. I sit. I wait. I flip the pages to Mark 6.

There are two big stories that happen side by side in Mark 6. The first is the story of the beheading of John the Baptist. It's a gruesome story, followed by another story that's better in my eyes: the feeding of the five thousand. The placement of these two stories is strange. You go from a *Game of Thrones* scene to a carb party. There's no intermission.

I think this has to be a mistake, but I know it isn't because I'm led to the other books of the gospels where the same stories are told. I am not someone who memorizes where stories are located throughout the Bible, so I know this is no coincidence. I dig back into Mark 6. I ask, *Why? What am I missing?*

I read the stories several times. I eventually give up and close the book.

The following day, I meet up with a reader attending the conference I'm speaking at. Her name is Sara. She asks what I'm planning to do with my next few days in Texas.

"I'll probably just be in my room writing. I have a lot of writing to do."

"Where will you eat?" she probes.

"I'm not sure," I say. "Honestly, I stopped at a drugstore earlier and got a can of soup, popcorn, a few oatmeal packets, and a teabag. I should be good."

Most people would see a trip to a new city as a chance to go out, explore, and try all the local cuisine. I prefer to hunker down in my hotel room and only venture out to the gym or the hotel restaurant.

"I'm Southern," she says. "Like, real Southern. Like, so Southern I can't handle the thought of you not eating real food.

"And if you've never had them before in Texas, you need to try the breakfast tacos. Will you let me bring you food tomorrow morning?"

"I'm good," I tell her. "Really."

"Please?"

I learned in my college years never to turn down free food when people offer it to you. I've learned in the South never to turn down free food ever. I've learned in Texas never to turn down breakfast tacos.

I give in and say yes.

Sara shows up the next morning. She has a navy dress on, pressed for a day of interviews, and her name tag is hanging around her neck. She holds in her fist a brown bag packed with bacon-and-egg breakfast tacos.

We sit together and eat. I make a dozen comments about how fluffy the tortillas are. We end up talking about Mark 6, how I can't seem to be released from the passages.

Sara majored in religion and has a master's degree in psychology. I'm thinking she is a good source to tell me what she thinks is the purpose of these two stories.

"I think it's pretty obvious," she says to me. "You don't see it?"

No. I don't see it.

Sara proceeds to tell me there is a clear difference between the two stories sitting side by side. One is all about *fear*, and it leads to the beheading. The second story is all about *love*, and it leads thousands to become full.

"You were just talking about how you keep struggling with these lies of fear. When you let those lies take over, you figuratively lose your head. You're defenseless. You're not fighting, and eventually, they'll kill you. But when you find a way to silence the lies and focus on love over fear, look what happens: That love overflows to the benefit of others. Miracles happen. Thousands of people get fed."

I go back to the Bible that afternoon and reread the stories. Sara is right. The first story is completely driven by fear. It's like fear is holding the pen. The second story is interesting because it begins with fear, but after a dramatic turnaround, it ends with love. At first, the disciples are tired and really afraid because they're sure there's no way they can ever feed a crowd this big. Jesus remains calm and tells the disciples to count what they have. He then proceeds to multiply it. He takes their fear and transforms it into love. I'm thinking Jesus could do this miracle all on his own, but he takes the extra time to calm their anxiety and empower each of them to break up the miracle and do their part.

What is even cooler than that is the tiny line at the end of the story. If you don't look closely, you'll miss it: "They all ate and were satisfied, and the disciples picked up twelve basketfuls of broken pieces of bread and fish." Translation: there were leftovers.

I think that's what happens when we choose love over fear. With love, there's always more left over. Fear shrinks and shrivels. Fear has an expiration date. But love keeps on growing, keeps on giving, with more than enough for everyone.

I say all of this because no matter how brave we get, it's still easy to go back to the story that fear wants to write for us. It's comfortable. We know all the words. It would be easy to just run back.

When it came to the love story of Lane and me, I was wishy-washy because of fear and that familiar story line. I would be all-in one day and wanting to bolt the next. Running away had nothing to do with Lane or who he was. I was just afraid. And fear and love had an all-out throwdown in my heart for some time.

One day I bought two journals at a bookstore. I gave one to Lane and kept one for myself. In the weeks that followed, he and I wrote notes and letters to one another. We'd exchange notebooks. Our love grew between the pages. I liked the notebooks because every time I sat down to write, I felt like I was deliberately choosing love over fear. I made my love into an action step. I think love was always meant to be an action step.

That first time we exchanged journals, I sat in my car and read every one of Lane's words to me. There was a note from March 18, 2016. On this day, I remember freaking out and starting a fight while talking to Lane on the phone. I told him I was afraid of marrying the wrong person. Note to self: Don't tell the guy you're dating that you're afraid of marrying the wrong person. Yet the fear was overwhelming, and I just wanted to be honest.

I was crying so hard, thinking it would all be taken away from me if I blinked. Lane was calm and steady on the other side of the phone. He stayed. I found out weeks later, as I read the journal, that he went to Taproom and wrote me a letter after we got off the phone.

"I feel like all your life you've let the fear of negative outcomes drive you to where you are now, but it also hasn't allowed you to experience true love," he wrote. "True love is not what our culture says. I'm talking about the true love that God shows, which is fully sacrificial, forgiving, and servant-hearted. I think those are the three qualities love should resemble.

"I know you love me, but today I've been scared you'll just run because it's easier (I don't actually think it's easier in the long run. It just appears that way)," he continued. "If you were to run down the road, all those things you ran from will just come back again."

Emmet Fox writes, "Fear destroys the body, kills inspiration, paralyzes business, throws a winter of death over everything."[1] Love is always creative, and fear is always destructive.

On the days when I get really fearful, I say a tiny prayer. It's called a breath prayer. During a series my pastor in Connecticut taught on the Beatitudes, he taught us how to say breath prayers—short, gritty prayers that get right to the point. You can say them anywhere and in any posture. You simply pick a sentence, something that looks like a prayer, and repeat it under your breath over and over again. Not long after, the breath prayer makes a little space in your heart and stays there.

I love the idea of breath prayers. There are plenty of times when I can't find the words or don't have the energy to get on my knees and pray. There are even times when I feel like my prayers aren't good enough, as if God won't meet me in my mess. There are days when I feel like every word that comes out of my mouth is fake or forced. Breath prayers help me bridge the gap between praying sometimes and praying without ceasing.

My breath prayer for when fear tries to take back the lead role is simple: *Reduce me to love.*

I can't take credit for making this prayer up. I hear it one morning as I pray with a group of volunteers at my church. I had signed up to work at a conference for worship leaders who came from all over the country to rest, refuel, and get inspired.

Before the doors open on the second morning, our group huddles close and links arms. The woman in the center begins to pray. At one point, she says it. "Reduce me to love. God, reduce me to love."

---

1. Emmet Fox, *Make Your Life Worth While* (New York: Harper, 1943), 37.

After we say amen, we get into place at the doors. Our job is to welcome the worship leaders and get them pumped for the full day ahead. I'm still not certain why anyone would think to give me this sort of job. I only make things more awkward when I am left to greet strangers. I'm that person who welcomes someone into the building and asks, "Is this your first time at church?" They give me the stink eye when they tell me they've been attending for four years. I've since retired from greeting people and now deliver coffee and bagels to the other people serving on a Sunday. It's easier to talk to bagels than to people.

I start saying hello to people as they come in the doors. Some look tired. Some look caffeinated. Some look like members of the band One Direction, and some look like Jesus.

A man walks toward me with stringy gray hair. He has his arms stretched out as if he has known me for years, as if this is our family reunion and he's my uncle. I looked at his name tag: Gino.

Gino and I hug like it's second nature. He pulls out his harmonica and begins playing "Amazing Grace" in the middle of the lobby as if no one else were there.

"What'll you have me play?" he asks.

I request the song "Danny Boy." He plays it, and I close my eyes for a minute. The song makes me think of my grandmother. It was one of her favorites. I can still hear her exclaiming over how much she loved that song.

Gino finishes his song. He places his hand on my shoulder and looks at me.

"Just remember to look beneath the surface," he says, his voice low. "Beneath the surface, we all just want to be seen. Every single one of us just wants to be seen."

As he says those words and slips past me into the crowd, that simple prayer comes back to me: *Reduce me to love.* When fear is leading, I miss these moments.

My prayer expands and gets bigger as I say it more: *Reduce me to love. Help me to see beneath the surface. Help me to be a familiar face in a crowd, a light in a dark room. Turn me into love and wipe out all the excess fear.*

The prayer is not asking that I'll be propelled into something bigger for this world. The prayer is "reduce." Make me smaller. Help me get out of my own way.

It's a classic John B kind of prayer. In John 3, John the Baptist says flat-out, "I'm not it. I'm not meant to be the center of attention." He tells his disciples that he was sent ahead to prepare the way for the bridegroom. "He must become greater; I must become less" (John 3:30).

My heart needs this reminder constantly: You are not the center of the universe. You are not the most important. That's God. If I want to be open to what God has for me, I also must be open to decreasing, to becoming less. I stick close to writer Flannery O'Connor's words in her prayer journal: "Dear God, I cannot love Thee the way I want to. You are the slim crescent of a moon that I see and my self is the earth's shadow that keeps me from seeing all the moon . . . Please help me to push myself aside."[2]

The world doesn't tell us a story about reduction. It tells us to be front and center, always impressive. The gospel is a different story. Gospel-living requires us to get smaller as we go, so that God can be amplified. Smallness is where the real work happens.

---

2. Flannery O'Connor, *A Prayer Journal* (New York: Farrar, Straus and Giroux, 2013), 3.

Smallness is where we learn what we're made of. Smallness is where our actions trump our words.

Reduce me to love. It's me saying, "I can't actually do this reduction thing on my own, so come in and do the work. Have your way. I trust you."

It's beautiful because I went a really long time without ever trusting God. My prayers were prayers that I could handle things and that I could see with my own strength. Now I like to pray for impossible things because I want to get to the end of my life and be able to say, "I saw impossible things, and the fear didn't win."

STEAL THIS PRAYER

Dear God, wipe out my fear and reduce me to love. Instead of constantly screaming out my narrative, I want you to point yours out to me in the lives of people around me. Let me feed people with hope and love instead of letting fear feed off of me. I want love to be the center of my story.

THANK YOUR LIMP

Chapter
Nineteen

I joined a gym down the street from where I live in Atlanta. It's a small gym. Nothing really impressive—just some weight machines, a few spin bikes, and a wall of cardio machines. When you sign up for the membership, you get a free session with a personal trainer. This is meant to sucker you into buying more sessions with the trainer. I reluctantly sign up for my session after enough harassment from one of the trainers who likes to correct my form on nearly every exercise.

On the day I go to meet him for the session, I am nervous. I want to prove myself. And while I am trying to impress him, I start to get the feeling he's hitting on me as we warm up on the StairMaster. He keeps making these comments about how he is a forty-year-old man and about how someone like me could only ever be with someone above the age of forty. It's getting weird, but then he stops and looks at me.

"You know," he says, "you remind me of a buffalo."

I have to do my best to not fall off the StairMaster at this point. Clearly I was deceived to believe he was into me. This is not a pickup line. You should never try to gain a person's interest by comparing them to a massive, grass-feeding animal.

Still, I was nothing short of intrigued.

"Tell me more."

"Well, buffalo are not like a lot of other animals." He branches out into a question. "What do you think is an animal's first instinct when they notice a storm is coming through?"

"I think they probably hide," I answered after a few seconds. "Yes, I think that's the natural inclination—to hide."

"Exactly! Most animals hide. We go inside. We find shelter," he said to me. "But the buffalo are different. They see a storm on the horizon, and they know they aren't going to escape the storm. They make a split-second decision and choose to run toward the storm instead of away from it. They charge into the storm so they can come out on the other side sooner.

"You don't seem like the kind to back off easily," he says, smirking as he powers down the machine to lead me into the weight room. "You seem like the kind to run into the storm."

"You'd be correct," I tell him. No hesitation. "You have no idea how correct you are."

We move through the workout together, but I find myself thinking about buffalo the whole time. I will likely find some buffalo wallpaper and redo my bedroom. I want a buffalo bedspread and a buffalo paperweight. I will name my first child "Buffalo." I want to be a buffalo more than anything else in the world.

I share this buffalo story with many people. I am like Oprah the moment she gave cars to the entire audience, except I'm passing out the role and title of "buffalo" to all my friends. "And you get to be a buffalo! And you get to be a buffalo!" I find myself exclaiming.

And then, a few weeks later, I walk into the gym to see the same trainer talking with another woman on the same StairMaster. He's telling her about buffalo. I realize in that moment that this man likely makes a living telling unassuming young women that they are in the bison family. Turns out, I'm not the only buffalo in that gym. It is a gym full of buffalo.

But maybe that's not the worst thing in the world. Maybe that's this trainer's calling in life. Maybe he knows the only way he can motivate someone to work for what they want is to start by telling them how brave and strong he already thinks they are. Maybe we all need someone to come along and say, "Hey, I know you think you can't do this, but guess what . . . you are capable of running into that storm and coming out on the other side. You're a buffalo; now go out there and prove it to the world."

Sometimes we need a new identity like that. A new name. Something that will push us to remember where we came from and then choose not to give up when the next hurdle comes along.

My thoughts turn to something that happened a few weeks before I dubbed myself a buffalo. It was that same summer, and I was five months into planting my roots in Atlanta. Somehow, someone at church thought it would be a good idea to invite me to summer camp and have me be in charge of four tenth-grade girls. Now when I say summer camp, I do not mean some bug-infested cabin with massive inflatable blobs that propel you into the middle of a murky lake. This is summer camp with hotel rooms on the beach and an extra helping of Jesus.

At the camp, one of the leaders needed some support with a camper who was experiencing a lot of anxiety about getting out of bed. I offered to meet with the girl in the hotel lobby before dinner that evening. I thought maybe I'd be able to give her some advice.

The girl's name was Hannah. We sat in the lobby to talk. Hannah has struggled with anxiety and depression for the last few years, like I have. She is seventeen.

At one point, I asked Hannah, "Do you know what our name means?"

"I think it means peace or grace or something like that," she said.

"I used to think that too."

I told her about my depression, about how during that time I became enamored with the story of Jacob in the Bible. Jacob had a twin named Esau. He was born after Esau and never really lived it down. Esau was the apple of his father's eye; Jacob was basically Jan Brady in man form.

Jacob isn't a walk in the park. He's annoying and conniving, and he lives up to the name his parents gave him at birth. The name Jacob meant "he grasps the heel." Jacob does a lot of shady stuff and ends up stealing his brother's birthright. At that time, a birthright was a pretty big deal. It was like mega ultra platinum status on Delta.

There is a pivotal moment in the middle of Genesis when Jacob is about to see his brother after all these years. He's terrified. He has no idea how his brother will receive him. So while traveling to meet him, Jacob sends his wife, kids, and all their stuff across a brook, and he stays behind for a night. I like to imagine this is the point when Jacob is like, "I'll catch up to you. I've got to handle a few things first."

The text says more than that though. Almost out of nowhere, this random man shows up, and he and Jacob begin to wrestle.[1] My mom and I make frequent comments about how strange this

---

1. Genesis 32:22–32.

is. I mean, how many times have you been on a run to Starbucks or the grocery store and suddenly get sidetracked by some dude wanting to wrestle you in the road?

Even stranger, the guy is rumored to be God. Commentaries differ on whether this wrestler was God, a man, or an angel. Regardless of the identity, the two wrestle until daybreak, and just when it seems like Jacob is going to win, the man touches Jacob's hip softly and it's dislocated out of his socket.

Jacob is likely crying and cussing as he screams at the man, "I'm not going to stop fighting until you bless! Bless me!"

So the man calmly asks Jacob, while he probably has him in a headlock, "What is your name?"

"Jacob," he answers.

"No longer," the man says. "Your name will no longer be Jacob. From now on, it's Israel, which means God-wrestler, since you wrestled with God and you made it through."

The translation I made up in my head basically says, "You're solid, Jacob. I see you growing and I see you trying. I'm giving you a new name so you won't be defined by your past."

Sitting in the lobby with the other Hannah, I told her that throughout my depression, I'd sometimes pray that prayer: *God, give me a new name. Give me a new name.*

To be honest, I have no idea what I was expecting. I didn't need God to show up one day and say, "Hey, you're Karen now." I think I was really praying, *God, I need you to show me I am something other than this depression. I need to know that if I wrestle with you, I will make it through.*

And then one morning, in the midst of my breakdown, my prayer got answered. I remember it being five in the morning. I sat at my kitchen table reading 1 Samuel. The story of

Hannah is in this book of the Bible. Hannah is a woman who desperately wants a child and can't seem to conceive. She prays a beautiful prayer to God about how she will give the child to him. She becomes pregnant, and her son grows up to become a great leader.

I was named after the Hannah of the Bible. As I skimmed through the text, one line of the commentary identified the name Hannah with her intense weeping in 1 Samuel 1 and suggested the name evokes "declaring loudly."

I'd never read this before. I knew that Hannah meant "grace, favor" in Hebrew, but here it was, sitting right in front of me, a new interpretation to my name. "Declaring loudly" was the opposite of how I felt throughout that depression. In the moment when God gave Jacob a new name, I bet he didn't own it immediately. It probably took some time for the confidence to grow inside him.

"Your name means 'declaring loudly,'" I said to the girl Hannah.

"Declaring loudly?"

"Yes," I said. "That's your new name. I don't know if that's ever happened to you, or if I can even give you a new name in a hotel lobby, but I am."

With tears in her eyes, Hannah said to me, "It's been 150 days."

"150 days?"

"150 days without self-harming. I've gone 150 days, but I still wake up every day in fear that I'm going to choose cutting again. I'm afraid I'll have to start all over."

"How do you keep track of the days?" I asked her.

"I just remember them. In my head."

I pulled out my notebook and ripped a page from it. As I wrote, I told her a story about my friend Nate. He was someone I really looked up to, a person whose life ended too swiftly. For thirty months, Nate fought against cancer, and in so many ways, he won the battles.

There was a chalkboard wall in my bedroom where I was living at the time Nate passed away. In the days that followed his passing, I took a piece of white chalk and made a tally board on it with two columns. In one column, I wrote the word CHOICE. In the other column, I wrote the words NO CHOICE. Nate taught me the importance of making choices every single day. As long as you're alive, you have choices you can make. You can either seize the day, or you can let the lies and the fear run you in circles until you're exhausted.

I started making tallies in the chart. For me, it was about wanting to get up early to do a workout—to start my day the right way before heading to the train to go to work. Every morning I woke up to the sound of the alarm and didn't go back to sleep, I'd put a tally on the CHOICE side because I'd made a solid choice to take control of my morning.

Every morning I ignored the alarm and went back to sleep, I wouldn't make a tally. The thing is, there's never a day when I have "no choice." I simply decide if I will use it or if I won't.

I draw out the same chart for her. I write CHOICE on one side and NO CHOICE on the other. I draw 150 choices on the side of the chart that reads CHOICE. I write at the top of the page YOUR NAME MEANS DECLARING LOUDLY.

"You've made 150 choices so far," I tell her. "You can look at this every day as a reminder when you're wondering if it's worth it, if it would just be easier to go back to cutting."

I tell her to mark a tally every single day she makes it without going back to cutting. I tell her she isn't alone. There are many days when I wake up and think I might tumble right back into the depression, but there is a different story I must choose to believe in. I need to choose the different story daily.

A few months later, I heard from Hannah again. She sent me a message with an attached photo of the chart we'd made together. I could see where my tally marks ended and hers began. She told me she was at 210 days—210 days of not cutting. The tallies may seem small at first, but they stack up. They remind us on days when we feel weak or tempted to give in again to the fear we thought kept us safe that we have come so far. The past doesn't get to define us anymore or whisper a false name into our ears.

There's another crazy factor in the Jacob story that I love. After he gets the new name, the text says Jacob walked with a limp for the rest of his life. God did some eternal dislocation of Jacob's hip, and because of that wrestling match, Jacob gained a limp. I imagine that if I had a limp, I'd probably go around talking about it. I would at least tell people I casually wrestled God one time on my way to a family reunion and this limp was sort of like a souvenir. Or I may have learned to complain about the limp—to look at it and be unable to keep myself from saying, *You are holding me back. You are keeping me from moving into all the places where I want to move.*

But that's not Jacob. You never see him screaming at God or begging for healing. For the rest of his life, he walks with this limp, but he never mentions it. I know he felt the limp every single day. It had to be a reminder to him, like, *Wow, I've wrestled with God. I came out knowing he was for me. He was for me, and look at how far he went to make sure I never forget he's with me.*

I think we all have a limp like Jacob's. Depression is mine. Every single day, I am aware of it. I see it. I remember the limp when I take my medication each morning or when I have a hard day that makes me want to curl up in a ball and give up. But that depression, no matter how much it tries to put its stamp on my life, does not get to define me. It's my proof I wrestled with God, my proof that he never left me in the dark.

We see Jacob one last time in the book of Hebrews. My man Jacob makes a triumphant return in the part of the Bible that's basically the "Who's Who of Faith." There's this line: "By faith Jacob, when he was dying, blessed each of Joseph's sons, and worshiped as he leaned on the top of his staff" (Hebrews 11:21). In the last sentence written about Jacob in this faith chronicle, it mentions him holding on to his cane because of that limp.

His limp was always there, but it clearly wasn't holding him back.

In the months that come after my depression, each one making it look smaller in the rearview mirror, I learn to talk about my own limp.

I meet up with Nick, the director of the college group I volunteer with at church, and he asks me to share my story with the four hundred students.

"I want you to talk about this last year if you're comfortable with it," he says. "I know what you walked through, and I think other people should know it too. You think you can talk about it?"

"I think I'm ready," I say, though there is hesitancy in my voice. "But do you think it will resonate? Do you actually think people need this message?"

"All I know is that I feel like this is the story that needs to be shared. And if you're ready, let's map it out."

We sat together and mapped out the story of depression from start to finish. What I liked most about mapping out my story with Nick was that he constantly stopped along the way and asked, "And where was God in this? Where did you see Jesus in this?" When we are in the dark and doing our best to just walk through it, I don't think there are many moments when we stop and recognize the bigness of God and the hand he's playing in our journey. But looking back and retracing the story, I had this unexplainable clarity that this is actually God's story and not my own.

I spoke to the college group a few nights later. I remember being nervous, afraid the message would be too much for people. They would think I was crazy. They would think I was unworthy to sit there and talk about the faithfulness of God.

When I looked out into the crowd that night, I realized I was wrong. Once again, I was wrong about what God wanted to do with me. My story may actually have been too relatable.

I had more real conversations with people that night than ever before. There were crazy moves of God and weeping. I prayed with several college students that evening, and they were some of the realest prayers I said in a long time. I laid my hands on their shoulders. I approached the situations with the biggest amount of faith I could muster up.

I learned that night that a lot of us are standing in the dark and don't know how to talk about it, so it's pertinent to start finding a way to talk about it. People can't find you if they don't know where to look.

This culture makes it really easy to act like we are doing

okay, to act like our lives are perfect and polished and one small step away from completion. In reality, we are lonely and we are grabbing for things. We are jealous and we are comparing ourselves to others more now than ever before. We are restless and we are discontented. I think social media is a beautiful thing, but I also think it allows us to fake being okay when we really aren't. I think it zaps away this space that used to exist where we could talk honestly and openly and not get distracted from our pain and the pain of others.

A lot of us are faking, and we're doing a good job of it. And while it's easy to blame social media, we need to be the ones who take the action steps. Technology will not stop advancing. The whole world isn't going to shut off. We have to be the ones to work harder, here and now, to find one another in the sea of screens and status updates. We have to be willing to have honest conversations, to meet up in person, to call each other (even when we don't feel like it) and ask the hard questions: "Are you okay? Are you okay, really? What's been going on? How do I pray?"

And here's just a little bit of advice that I've learned along the way. You don't have to take it. But if you ask someone, "How do I pray for you?" and they give you an answer, then actually pray. There are too many of us who say, "I'll be praying for you," and then never give that person a second thought. Even if you think your prayers are ineffective and don't matter to God, still pray.

When you talk about your limp, something cool usually happens. People get more honest. They open up about their own hard stuff. We learn to rally with one another and not be defined by our weaknesses. Our weaknesses become a bridge instead of a roadblock. We become little light holders on that bridge, helping other people find their way out of the dark.

It's beautiful to be light to someone else. We get the chance every day, even if we don't see it. But light is only powerful because it has known the darkness before.

STEAL THIS PRAYER

Dear God, take my limp and turn it into a lighthouse. I want my story to lead to hope and help others come out of the woods.

| Chapter Twenty | # COME MATTER HERE |

I make a friend in Atlanta who is a few years older than me. She is someone who prays fiercely, and God gives her pictures. God lets her see stuff that other people may never see. She told me she had a vision of me one day as she was praying for me. I was standing in the middle of a big crowd blowing bubbles. She said that at first I was blowing big bubbles that were very impressive to the crowd. However, the big bubbles popped quickly. Eventually I began blowing tiny bubbles, and the small bubbles floated above the crowd and reached even more people. The smaller bubbles had much more of an impact than the bigger ones.

When she told me this, I thought back on the last year and laughed to myself. I wanted to be the rooted one. I wanted to be steady, the kind of person someone could go to if they needed a prayer. I wanted to be the person who stayed, not the one who reached for the suitcase every time life got hard or people disappointed me. I did the work to get there.

I didn't get to have it all right immediately. There was a process involved and a road to take. That's how I realized how much I loved the smaller bubbles, the tiny things we all get to do to make our presence known to the people we love. At some point, we're faced with the choice to swap being impressive for being deliberate with the people around us.

225

This last year, I was having lunch in Atlanta with a guy who was a coworker at one of my first jobs after college. We'd both been the "fairly new millennials" on staff. When I left my job there, and shortly after that left the state, Michael had taken a different route. He began traveling around the world to different areas where our nonprofit was at work on the ground.

I couldn't keep track of him after a while. He was busy and owning it. I'd get the occasional call from a past coworker, and somewhere in there would always be the words, "Where's Michael at these days?" He was coming and going, making his impact on the world.

Now he was here. In Atlanta. Looking at graduate schools and meeting up with me. It's crazy that I've been here long enough to call Atlanta my city now. I stayed. I made it my home.

We sat across from one another at one of my favorite brunch spots in the city. We rehashed old memories over bacon and eggs, and he asked me how I liked living here. Graduate school in the city was one possible plan for him; the other was going back to traveling and spending some more time in high-risk foreign countries. I couldn't imagine just "spending some more time" there.

I knew I probably wouldn't see him for another few months after this as he went off the grid on some new adventure. I couldn't help but see how different our lives looked from the outside. He was going and exploring; I was rooted and learning how to chop vegetables and feed a tiny basil plant. Both were adventures in their own rights.

As he talked about leaving again, I started to wonder about

him. I wondered how hard it was to plant your roots, to feel like you belonged somewhere, when you were always leaving.

"Do you think maybe you're running from something?" I asked. I can easily become a therapist over brunch if you allow me to.

"Running from something?" he said. "Oh no, you are asking the wrong question." He's amused by me. He has always been a lot more confident than me.

"How?" I asked.

"The question isn't, 'What am I running from?' The better question is, 'What am I running toward?'"

He didn't give it a second thought. To him, he wasn't running from anything. He was simply running toward something.

For a long time, I marked myself as a "runner" in my story. I was someone who couldn't stop long enough to see the good all around her. I was someone who was always afraid of missing the point, so much so that I missed the present. It's crazy how I can so easily let fear tell me I'm running away, always running away, when maybe there's a different story beneath it. Maybe I was running toward something better all this time.

This has definitely been the best story I've gotten to live so far, though I can't place a bow on top of it and give it a happy ending or make it sound more complete than it really is. I'm not looking for that anymore. This story will keep going. I'm done with thinking I will "arrive someday" and that arrival will somehow fuel my completion. I'm already here.

Pivotal moments are happening every day. Lane helps me learn this. We are choosing one another daily, and I am learning with each choice that love shows you all you have to work at and all you want to be. Two people get to partner in that trek toward "better versions of ourselves," and the outcome has the potential to be really remarkable. I told my friend the other day that real love was nothing like I thought it would be. I thought love would be like taking a dozen pictures of yourself (which we've all probably done) in the hope of picking the most desirable portrait to give to someone. Turns out, real love is actually taking all the photos that are less desirable and really a little scary and handing them over to someone, saying, "Here. You get all of me. You get the ugly and the beautiful. Please stay."

When we give up the desire to "arrive," we start to see other elements of the story. We see hope show up in place of discontent. I saw that this year as Lane and I got engaged and started planning a wedding. Like it was scheduled all along, I was revisited by all the fear that my depression would come back. I was afraid it would steal my life once again. Lane was calm.

"People say all the time that God doesn't do the same miracles now that he used to do in the Bible," he tells me one night. "But people aren't looking close enough. People are discounting what a miracle looks and sounds like. I think it's a modern-day miracle that doctors can create medication that balances the chemicals in the brain."

He tells me I'm witnessing a miracle firsthand, if only I open my hands and receive it. It is a miracle that I can be prescribed something that lifts my fog of depression and allows me to seek God doggedly and serve him persistently. It is my own modern miracle to feel the depth of my relationships, take in the love of my fiancé, and renew my mind without a million detour signs running in my brain.

Instead of tumbling back into that old, familiar fear, we took a proactive step. I parted ways with the doctor who originally prescribed my medication and made an appointment to see a doctor who would integrate faith and mental health into one conversation. It doesn't seem like the most exciting appointment to schedule in the midst of arguably better ones—dress fittings, food testing, and meetings with a wedding planner.

"Have you read the book of Job?" my new doctor asks during our first meeting.

"I have in pieces," I say. "It was my favorite for a while, but people told me to lay off it while I was going through the depression because it was a little too intense."

"Well, how did it end for Job?" she asks.

"I know he had a lot of awful things happen to him. But his life was restored in the end."

"Yes," she says, "but it would never go back to what it was. And for Job, it was never about whether his life would be restored or not. He learned how much God loved him."

We always talk about the restoration of Job's life, how the blessings came back to him. How there was a calm after his storm.

"I bet Job still cried at night though," I say to her. "I bet Job still felt the pain of loss. I bet people said to Job all the time, 'Well look, God restored it in the end.'"

If I were Job, I would probably look at them and say, "Yes, but you don't know how much I value the taste of air. The taste of breathing after a long time of drowning." When you've been through hell and back, you never take the taste of air for granted again. It's with you every day. You suck it in and you exhale graciously.

She tells me that one-third of people go on medication, come off it, and never have to go back on it again. Another third go on medication, come off it, and have to go back on it when symptoms return. The final third are on it for their entire lives, and that's okay too.

I've never had a doctor tell me "that's okay too" with regard to mental health and medication. Words like "that's okay too" mean everything to me. I'm okay too. That's all I needed to hear.

My new doctor lets us close with a prayer. It's not short and rushed. It's long, leisurely, and winding. She cares about the words. I've never had prayer in a doctor's office before.

As I leave her office with new answers, I'm laughing to myself. I remember how I used to pray constantly throughout my depression that I would just see God. Turns out, he was hiding in plain sight. I had to adjust my vision, see things differently, to realize he was there all along. He was there in the faith and in the un-faith, like the moment you find Waldo right under your nose.

I've changed. I have something now that I didn't have before. Now I have eyes that see in the dark. This is by far the most beautiful part of my diagnosis. Some days are still hard. Some mornings are still slow and threatening. The threats are empty though, because I know the way home now. I have eyes that see in the dark, and they don't run from the thought of returning to that dark place. I know the dark cannot have me anymore.

You'll change too. It's inevitable. I don't know where you'll go or how you'll get there. We all want different things. You might spend your life traveling around the world to great parks and great cities. You might spend your life in one house, raising a family that is impossibly bold. You may pick up every six months and go somewhere new. No one is going to be able to stop you from these choices. But I'll tell you what I know: There is a difference between running from something and running toward it. Fear owns one of those stories, and I don't want him to think he has permission to mishandle yours.

So here are my hopes for you. You and I have traveled far enough together that I feel like it's only right to leave you with some traveler words for whatever comes next. Do what you want with them. Highlight what you love or rip out the page to take with you. These are just the prayers I'm saying this morning for you.

I hope your story involves the shattering of some comfort zones. My comfort zone exploded into a million bedazzled pieces when I moved, and while I hated to see it break at that time, I'm thankful I've never been able to put it back together.

I hope you fall in love with cities, coffee shops, people, and good books. I hope you fall in love with your place in this world. People always told me love was quick and instant. I was afraid to blink, because *what if I missed it?* But I don't want to tell you the same thing. I don't think it's all instant or quick. You will fall in love with people, cities, jobs, and prospects in an instant, but after that, the hard work of staying in love will remain. Dig in. Don't be afraid of that. There's all sorts of gold in learning how to stay in love after the magic wears off and the fireworks stop exploding.

There is great magic in the ordinary. I wish I had seen it years before this, but I'm thankful I have it now. There's magic in the friends who bring you flowers for your new home and the friends who know you're doing some crazy "no grain, no dairy, no anything edible" diet and they cook you something to make you feel included. There is magic in the people who pat the space beside them on the couch and tell you to come sit. They lay their hands on you and pray big prayers for you. They talk to God about you and it's beautiful, because they know you and they know God too.

There is magic in the people who see you with no makeup on. In the ones who answer their phone at three in the morning, throw on a sweatshirt, and drive straight over to you. They're there in the crisis mode and they don't leave you alone.

There is magic in quiet mornings when it's just you, a cup of coffee, and a book you can spend your whole life trying to figure out. They call this thing faith. They call this thing love. It doesn't come with a map or a manual. It will be a daily fight to make it your own. But there is so much good in sticking with something and not giving up. I hope you learn that faith isn't a thing to check off a list; it's a lifelong pursuit. As the good man Eugene Peterson says, it's a "long obedience in the same direction."[1]

Don't run from this stuff. Run toward it with everything you have.

While I don't hope that something comes along to break your heart, I know it inevitably will. And so, when the storm hits and the darkness tries to win, I hope you remember that your spirit is made of something thick and durable. You're a fighter, and no one gets to take that from you. The darkness doesn't get to have you. I hope you never get too scared to speak out your story. Your story isn't a burden; it's a healing balm. May God use it to fix and restore, encourage and revive.

I hope you say yes to the things that scare you. I hope you say sorry when sorry is due. I hope you don't ghost people.

1. Eugene Peterson, *A Long Obedience in the Same Direction* (Downers Grove, IL: InterVarsity, 1980).

I hope you become a respecter of stories you don't understand and ask all your questions while you have the time and space. Accept invitations to art shows and cooking classes. Say yes to Tinder dates and learn how to pray. We're all in a club we never talk about, this club with no meetings called "trying the best we can." We all have badges and stripes of honor in this club. We all have a lifetime membership.

I hope you walk in everyday life and see Jesus in the people who bundle up your groceries and drive you to the airport. I hope you take the time to cultivate the things of this lifetime that matter more than instant success or acclaim. Love. Faith. Trust. Hope. Resilience. These take time. I hope instead of just settling for being known on the surface, you let people in, that you allow them to see the many parts of you. I hope the people who are meant to stay, stay. I hope you're not a spectator in the lives of other people. Be in the stories. Help people draw the maps. Show up, show up, show up.

More than anything, I hope you know how much it matters that you're here. You're not waiting to arrive. There are people who need you. There are churches that need you. There are miracles waiting in the wings for all of us, but we have to be able to wake up and see them. There's no reason for them to come sauntering onto the stage if we aren't in the audience, attentive and ready.

If I am on my phone, I miss it. If I am stuck inside my head, I miss it. If I am handing over my boarding pass to fear, I miss it. I miss what God is doing in the mundane, and I miss the chance to play a role in the love story he is writing.

There's a voice in my brain that is solid and eager to assure that there is something greater for me and for all of us out there.

233

It is only confident like this because I am training myself to remember the truth above the lies. The voice reminds me that the point is not to run myself ragged chasing after things I think will fill the hole. The point is not to worship the destination and miss all the dotted lines in between.

I think the point of this lifetime is to live as deeply as you can, with the people to the right and left of you, in the place where God sets your feet. The point of this lifetime is to become okay with saying, "Wherever I am—in waiting or in triumph—I know there is a purpose." Life isn't something we talk about; it's something we do.

It's so easy to go backward, to go right back to being the people who fear they'll never make a difference. To be the people who wait on the "come matter here" text to show up on their screen.

I hope you stop waiting on that text and realize the truth: It's already been sent. It was delivered hours ago. You are here, so don't miss it. You already matter, so don't be afraid to believe that. Come matter here. I've saved you a seat. Just come matter right here—where you already are, where the real magic happens.

STEAL THIS PRAYER

Dear God, show up, show up, show up.
And teach me to do the same.

ACKNOWLEDGMENTS

There was a time when I thought this book might never exist. Turns out, I had to live the story well before I ever sat down to write it. I am thankful, first and always, to God for bringing me through the hurdles and the challenges necessary to make this book a reality. This book would still be an idea if not for the people who made me walk the story before talking about it.

To Mom and Dad—thank you for never limiting me when it comes to dreams and ambitions. Mom, I've always wanted to follow in the footsteps of your journey, and I think this is the closest I've come yet. Dad, thank you for that time you dropped me off at the airport and gave me a hug, saying, "Don't take things too seriously." I needed that.

To my Grandmother Baccu—we're here again. We made it. I wish you could see this unfolding. Thank you for being the loudest cheerleader in my corner, even after all these years. This one, as well as every other book I write, is for you.

A sheet of gold stars should go to my husband, Lane, for all the coffee and breakfasts he made for me during this writing process. Belle—you're the most unexpected but greatest gift to come out of this story. Thank you for covering me in prayers and reminding me who I am.

I am a big believer that every author has an army of "make

it happen" cheerleaders behind her. I would not be here without mine.

I cannot imagine this road or any of my publications without my agent Mackenzie. M—you teach me to be fierce and keep me rooted. I love you.

I've had a blast this season working with my editor, Stephanie. She's the real mastermind in all of this. Stephanie—thank you for pushing me to be honest and to tell the truth. I've never looked so forward to hundreds of comments in the margins. You remind me through every edit why I love the craft of writing so much.

To the diligent souls at Zondervan who welcomed me in and made me feel like a part of the team—I'm honored to be a part of the work you're doing in the world. I pray this is just the start to the good projects we will create together.

To my sounding boards and unofficial editors—Blake, thank you for enduring hours of introspection with me. Jenna—thanks for the trips to Waffle House at midnight. Claire Biggs and Douglas—thanks for helping me find the diamonds-in-the-rough sludge pile we started with. Claire Flare—I could not do this work without you. Thanks for partnering with me. Kim—thanks for the 5 a.m. hours. Dawn and Brooke—thank you for helping me become myself fully throughout this writing process. I became someone new because of your love.

There are a number of people who lived the content of this book with me. Without them, I wouldn't have stories to tell.

To my church in Connecticut, in Atlanta, and the PCC college group—thank you for pushing me closer to God when the darkness felt immeasurable. To Chrisy, Carol, Nancy, Kate, and Kelly—thank you for teaching me how to stay. You are my constants, and I would not have been able to walk this road toward recovery without you. Thank you for always pointing me back to God.

Lindsey—thank you for telling me not to settle for some basic love story. I needed your tough love to get back in the oven and finish the work.

Eryn—so much of this journey happened because you believed I could move and make it happen. Thank you for being the push and for helping me find my place.

To the people of Rowsdower—you have been my purest and most constant form of community. Thank you for always showing up in the good and the bad. It seems only fitting to write: I'm like the moon.

To my communities in Atlanta, Connecticut, and beyond—I love this life with you. Thank you for teaching me that real friendship is honest and fun.

To Taproom Coffee—I'll forever be on a mission to be your most dedicated regular. Thank you for the coffee and the space to write and be myself.

Thank you to all the people who gave me the invaluable wisdom needed to create this book. Special thanks to Jeff Shinabarger, Jonathan Pasqual, and Hannah Rinehart for giving advice that served as pivotal turning points. Thank you to the people who held me in the in-between moments—Clifton, Caroline, Lindsey R., Jane, Joey, Karen, and Tiffany.

To a group of young women I believe in fiercely—Melissa Warten, Maddie Harkey, Delaney Strunk, Ashley Harris, Emily Dukes, Emily Thomas, Johanna Pendley—you are fire for the next generation. Always be loud, always be bright, and never apologize for it.

And to my readers—you are the best in the world. Really. Thank you for cheering me on and believing I could bring this work out into the world. You are my inspiration, and I'm in awe of you and the shoes you walk in every single day. My inbox is always open for you. Let's keep building bright fires and creating beautiful things together.